THE *Other* WOMAN

L. S. TOPPING

THE Other WOMAN

shero Publishing
SHEROPUBLISHING.COM

Publishing/Editing: SHERO Publishing
Graphics & Cover Design: Greenlight Creations Graphics Designs
glightcreations.com/ glightcreations@gmail.com

Table of Contents

Author DEDICATION

To my beloved children and my dearest husband, you have been my rock, my inspiration, and my greatest blessings. Your unwavering love and support have carried me through the highs and lows of this journey. I am endlessly grateful for the laughter, the hugs, and the endless encouragement you have given me.

To my friends and family, your presence in my life has been a source of strength and comfort. Your support and belief in me have been a guiding light. I am deeply thankful for your love, understanding, and unwavering support.

To the women reading this book, God's grace has been my sustenance, and His love has been my anchor. With faith as my guide, I hope that the story I share will resonate with you and give you the courage and hope that you need during your own struggles.

With all my love and gratitude,
Latoyoua Topping

INTRODUCTION

When I first said, "*I do*," I pictured a marriage of happiness and love, marked by the everyday triumphs and challenges of raising children and building a life together. Sure, I knew there would be ups and downs. But nothing prepared me for the storm that would turn my world upside down, pushing me to face betrayal, heartbreak, and the depths of resilience I didn't know I had. This is not just a story about infidelity and broken vows. This is a story about discovering the strength hidden in plain sight, a story of faith and the power of self-reclamation.

In my journey, I found a part of myself that had been dormant for far too long—the woman who could pick herself up after every fall. I faced my husband's betrayal and the heartbreak of an outside child, but I emerged from it not as a shadow of my former self, but as a woman made whole, fierce, and unapologetic. My scars no longer define me; they empower me. I've found an unwavering strength to prioritize my children and myself, to build a fulfilling life centered on my growth, my career, and my faith.

I thought my story would be one of love lost, but it's a tale of a *woman* found —the woman reborn through heartbreak, the one who refused to let her trials define her. This journey has been about rising from what was meant to break me and stepping into a purpose I had not envisioned. It is a testament to every woman who finds her voice, power, and self-worth amid life's storms. And with that, I welcome you to my story.

THE *Other* WOMAN

L. S. TOPPING

Chapter One

THE GIRL

THE GIRL

While many are thinking about their New Year's resolutions, studies have proven that most will probably fail before the month ends. On the other hand, I am putting my New Year's resolution into action. I felt stuck in my small hometown, yearning for new experiences and opportunities. So, I decided to move to Atlanta, Georgia. I packed my bags, said goodbye to my family and friends, and hopped in my car to start my new life in the city.

Atlanta is the core of the Civil Rights Movement and where critical individuals who played a significant part during that era resided. There are tremendous economic opportunities for young middle-class and upper-class African Americans. It was home to Freaknik (an annual spring break event for college students) and influential Historically Black Colleges and Universities (HBCUs). I may have been saying this to convince myself of the significant change. I will admit that I was anxious but excited at the same time. Who wouldn't be anxious and excited when making a huge life change in less than a month? I don't know if those two feelings exist simultaneously, but hey, I'm Trinity Jones, so why not?

I grew up in what some would call privileged in the suburbs of South Florida. However, I am here to tell you that my childhood was far from the allusion that so many believe. I am the oldest of five siblings. My mom's aunt raised us. She was a churchgoing, Bible-toting woman who played no games. We attended church three days a week. Also, we were stuck doing chores on Saturdays when the neighborhood kids were outside playing. Do not get me wrong, we did have a childhood. It was just with restrictions.

Although I was the oldest, my brothers had more freedom. I was monitored like a parolee on probation if I did something as simple as cross the street. I would be in trouble which would lead to me being grounded, more like house arrest. I could not wait for graduation to come. I would finally have the freedom to live a little. My aunt always said that if you lived in her house, you would abide by her rules, and going to church was one of those rules. Graduation felt like a lifetime away, but when it came, it felt like the Fourth of July. I could picture the fireworks and music celebrating the ankle monitor and brooms dropping. I am exaggerating, but you would have imagined graduating the same way if you had been in my shoes.

After graduating high school, I got accepted to Bethune Cookman College. It was more of my mom's dream to see me go to an HBCU. It did not matter to me where I went. I was so eager to proclaim my independence. It was not a girl gone wild type of freedom, but it was close. My first year at college was supposed to be about finding myself and being independent, but I met Jaxon and fell in love. At least, that is what I thought love was back then. Jaxon was much older than I was and already had four kids. Yep, I became an instant stepmother before enjoying the fruits of freedom. What was I thinking?

Nevertheless, it did not bother me because he was my boo thang. It still sounds corny to this day. Jaxon was also my first official boyfriend, and the best thing about it was I did not have to sneak around to be with him. My aunt was very strict about dating. I was not allowed to date, even as a senior in high school. If I was outside, and someone happened to walk by and stop to talk to me, she would make me come into the house quickly. From her reaction, you would have thought the boy, and I were caught doing something inappropriate.

Jaxon and I were in a serious relationship, which was very new to me. We would take trips and go to family functions together, all the things that couples do. We even played house; in other words, we lived together. So clearly, you can tell that I had a little more growing up to do. Looking back on it now, I needed more life experience before getting involved with someone eight years my senior with four kids. But none of that mattered to me back then. I was just a young girl in love with him, and he was into me.

Jaxon's demeanor was that of a gentleman with street swag, dreads, and gold teeth but not one tattoo. His smile was infectious—the opposite of the boys that I dated in high school. Yes, I had my share of boyfriends, but I had to sneak and date them. I liked to call them my school boyfriends because we only talked and hung out during school hours unless I snuck out. I now understand why good girls like bad guys; it is their confidence. They draw attention when they enter a room, and are aggressive but in a good way. It is like riding a roller coaster; the fun and excitement at the beginning of the relationship lead to unknown surprises and suspense. And just like that, it turns into heartaches and pain. Men like Jaxon have a lot of temptations thrown their way. It might not be as much as the pro athletes or celebrities, but more than the average guy. So, settling down is the furthest thing on their agenda.

Jaxon would take me on lavish trips and shopping sprees. He also bought me luxury cars. I will admit the perks and benefits were great, but it was something that I had to get used to. It was a part of why I felt so hard for him. I admit he made it hard for any contenders, but now that I look back on it, I realize it was more of an infatuation with the lifestyle he presented to me. One time, on one of our getaways, he proposed to me. The moment was intimate and unique. Despite the lavish lifestyle, he kept it quite simple. I was enamored by being engaged, and a year went by, and we still did not set a wedding date, nor did I ever think to mention it. Wow, he had me lost in his love.

The relationship got intense. Jaxon and I decided to move in together. This decision was a significant move, but I had no second thoughts. During the first month in our new place, Jaxon would take me to school and drop me off, which I did not mind. He used to tell me that he wanted the guys there to know that I was with him. And like a fool, I thought that was a sign of love. With all that confidence, he still was a little insecure. It was cute. He did not know how much I enjoyed him taking me and watching the looks of the other female students as I jumped out of a white Mercedes Benz sitting on 20-inch rims. My male classmate's perception of my relationship with Jaxon was that you had to have money to get with me. That could not have been the furthest from the truth. I was not a gold digger. When I met Jaxon, I did not know what he had. The conversation after an argument with my aunt drew me in.

What was supposed to be a happy time quickly turned into a nightmare. We were supposed to be sharing our home until I finished school. By no means was the plan for it to be Jaxon's part-time getaway retreat. I could have continued living in the dorm and used the extra money for my fun if I had known this would happen. I asked him several times when he planned to be here permanently or at least four to five days out of seven days of the week. There were constant excuses to explain why he could not be there. Lame ones like "I need to manage my business," blah, blah, blah. At home, he was always out in the clubs or traveling to some city for a football game, NOT WORK. I should have known better when the relationship started with lies and deception. I would not have built the courage to leave the relationship if it was not for his kids' mother.

It amazes me how so many of us continue letting someone take advantage of or abuse us because we are afraid to stand alone. A friend once told me she would not leave her cheating baby's father because she did not want another woman to get him if he stopped cheating. This fear of the unknown is gambling on the possibility of a what-if. My reason was that I did not want to lose the money and independence that came along with being with him.

The old saying, "What glitters is not always gold," is true. My aunt always called it polished brass.

What happened between Jaxon and me that gave me a completely new outlook on life, let alone moving to an entirely new state? Okay, he was not the reason for me to move, but it sounded good. Since you must know, here it is. One weekend, I decided to come home from college to spend time with my family and fiancé. I thought I would surprise him and wait until I got into town to tell him I was coming. Unfortunately, it was late, so I decided to wait until the next day. I tried calling him around noon, but there was no answer. I waited a while and tried several more times, but still no response. Jaxon's schedule was like clockwork, so he would have told me if he was traveling.

Therefore, around 8 o'clock, I decided to go out with friends for fun. We went out to one of Jaxon's usual spots, Diamonds Bar and Blue Lounge. I saw some of Jaxon's homeboys, but no Jaxon. Now, that was strange, and what made things even more bizarre was when I asked them if they had heard from him, they said *no*. These guys were like his minions, they knew where he was. So, I decided to creep out of the club and go to his sister's house to see if he was there.

As I pulled up to the house, I saw his car parked in the driveway, just like I figured. I was so focused on why he ignored me, but then I noticed his baby mama truck in the yard. As I knocked on the door, I could hear people talking, which was usual since everyone came to hang out at his sister's house. I could hear children playing in the living room. His sister had a glass window in her door, so I could see people walking around the house. Just as his son approached the door, I heard Jaxon say, "Go sit down. I will get the door". After what seemed like forever, he finally came to the door.

When he opened the front door, I could tell he was surprised. Then he had the nerve to ask, me what I was doing there. *"What am I doing here?"* I thought to myself. He had some nerve. Usually, he would have grabbed me and given me the biggest hug. But instead, he stepped out the door and closed it behind him quickly. Mind you, we had been together for almost three years; I used to live here with him, and oh yeah, we were engaged! I was taken aback by how he acted because I was trying to break it off the week before. After discovering some extracurricular activities, he adamantly denied, Jaxon begged me to stay in the relationship.

As we stood outside, as if I were some strangers, his baby mama came out of the house. I kept my composure because I did not want to give her the tiniest bit of satisfaction about how pissed I was. I knew the obvious, but I still had to ask the question. "Jaxon, what is this? What is going on?" He could not look at me. His baby mama chimed in for him to tell me what the deal was. With the look of an adolescent boy who just got in trouble, he said, "I think that I need to be with my family." My reaction was to say, "Oh, really, Jaxon?! So now you think that? What happened last week when I tried to leave? Don't worry about it. GOODBYE!" I turned around and walked off to my car, unbothered.

Although it hurt like hell, I refused to give them the satisfaction of seeing my pain. I couldn't believe he did that to me. And that day was the last day for Jaxon and me.

Chapter Two

NEW GIRL IN TOWN

Chapter Two
NEW GIRL IN TOWN

I hoped the ATL had something or someone better for me on the horizon, although I am not looking for anything. There is one downfall to Atlanta, though; the ratio of men to women is fifteen to one. That did not include the men searching for their Mr. Right. Mr. Right should have been the last thing on my mind, especially after the big breakup and calling off my engagement with Jaxon. A girl is not getting any younger. But trust me, the focus is on me.

The image flashback of that horrible day until the ringing of my phone startled me.

"Hello?"

"Hey Trinity, where are you? How much longer do you have before you are here?" the female voice on the other end of the phone demanded.

"Hey Nahla, I am okay. My GPS says I have three more hours until I make it to you."

"Oh, okay."

Nahla has been my best friend for over twenty years. She attended college in Atlanta and remained there after graduating.

"That is fantastic! I have so much planned for us when you get here," Nahla said excitedly.

Nahla kept talking, but I could only think about relaxing and showering. I was not in the mood to socialize. I had not seen Nahla in almost a year, and she sounded so enthusiastic that I did not want to hurt her feelings. So, Nahla talked about her plan for about twenty more minutes until my phone beeped.

"Hey Nahla, I have to go. I will call you back". I clicked over before Nahla could say okay.

"Hello, this is Trinity."

"Hello, Trinity, this is Mr. Bell," the deep voice on the other end of the phone replied.

"Hello, Mr. Bell; how can I help you," I ask.

"Trinity, I wanted to make sure you had a safe trip up here and confirm that you will be in the office on Monday at nine o'clock," Mr. Bell replied.

"Oh yes, Mr. Bell. I will be there on Monday, and my drive to Atlanta is going great. Thank you for asking," I answered.

"That's great, Trinity; I will see you on Monday. Goodbye", Mr. Bell said before hanging up the phone. I hung up, turned my music back up, and focused on my drive.

It's nothing but up from here, which is long overdue. I could not be more than thrilled about leaving the drama behind. The more I thought about it, the more excited I got. I turned the music louder and started singing like I was performing at my sold-out concert. The people in the passing cars probably think I am crazy, but oh well. As I got into the song, my phone rang, "UGH!"

"What is it now, Nahla?" I felt annoyed as I answered my cell phone.

"Hey baby, what are you doing?" a male voice on the other end of the phone asked. I know that voice from anywhere. It was Jaxon. Who was he calling, baby, and why was he calling me after what happened? It was seven months ago, but I was still in my feelings.

"I am en route to Atlanta, JAXON," I replied snarkily.

"Oh, you were serious about leaving. So you just up and leave me like that?" asks Jaxon.

Jaxon had a way with words to make it seem like it was the other person's fault.

"Jaxon, are you going to act like you had nothing to do with the end of our engagement? How about I paint a picture for you? Um, oh, me catching you in bed with your baby mama at your sister's house. Then you had the nerve to tell me you thought you needed to be with your family. Let's not forget you ignored my phone calls and lied about coming to get me, "I responded harshly.

"So, you are going to bring that up again," Jaxon replied.

I could tell from Jaxon's tone I touched a nerve.

I asked, annoyed, "Jaxon, what do you want? I need to focus on the road."

"Really, T? I was trying to see where you were so I could come and spend time with my baby, but you got up and left me", he responded immaturely. T is what close friends and family called me.

"Look, Jaxon, this conversation is not going anywhere. I gave you more times than you deserved and three abortions. But, like you said in front of your baby mama, you need to be with your family. So, I gave you that, and I am good over here. I wish you and your family well. Let me help you blame me for moving to another state. I'm cool with that because I am done with your cheating ass. I am cool with it. Goodbye".

I said sternly and then hung up the phone without waiting for his response. I cannot believe that I almost contemplated killing myself over him. Thank you, GOD, for getting me out of that situation.

About forty-five minutes later, I arrived at Nahla's townhouse. The bustling energy of the city immediately struck me. The skyscrapers towering above me, the sounds of cars honking and people talking, and the sight of the busy streets filled me with excitement. I made it just as the sun set behind her two-story brick townhouse in a trendy neighborhood. Nahla's neighbors were walking their dogs, and the kids were riding their bikes. As I step out of my 2018 black Audi and into the fall breeze, I quickly reach back into my car for my jacket because the fall evening air in Atlanta is more relaxed than the fall in Florida. Florida only has one season, Summer.

Nahla must have had a tracker on me or been sitting by her window because she came running out of the house immediately. She had an oblong face with angular cheekbones and a pointed chin. Nahla stood about 5'8" and 120 lbs, with butter pecan brown skin. She walked with long strides, her shoulders back and face held forward with a big, energetic smile. She was wearing purple bedroom shoes and a bright orange mini dress.

"Trinity, you made it," Nahla excitedly screams as she wraps her skinny arm around me.

"Yes, I'm here," I replied with fatigue in her voice.

Nahla's excitement overshadowed my fatigue because she immediately got into the plans for the night.

"Nahla, Nahla, calm down. How about you help me with my luggage," I said with a neutral tone.

As I walked into the townhouse, I noticed that Nahla's style had changed to a more contemporary style. Of course, I prefer a more modern one, but I am okay with whatever. I am just grateful that she is letting me stay with her.

"Come on, Trinity, let me show you your room!" To my surprise, the room had a modern vibe with neutral colors.

"So, what do you think?" Nahla asked.

As I lay across the king-size bed with my eyes closed, I said, "It's great!"

"Great! Get settled because the fun starts at nine o'clock. Lucy and Ethel are about to take over Atlanta." Nahla said as she left the room. Lucy was the main character in a popular 50s sitcom that my auntie and Nahla's mom would watch. Ethel was her best friend.

I glanced at the clock on the nightstand and realized it was in an hour. Ugh, all I want to do is rest from the long drive, unpack, and prepare for my first day at work just as I drift into a deep sleep.

"Trinity!" Nahla yelled.

Nahla's yelling startled me so much that I jumped out of my sleep, ready to fight. I had a flashback moment, but that is a story for another time and another place. Returning to reality, I stretched my arms to the ceiling and yawned.

"I'm up, I'm up. Give me thirty minutes, and I will be ready."

I usually liked to take my time getting dressed. Anything less than an hour meant I was not in the mood or could care less if I was cute. Forty-five minutes later, we were heading downtown.

Nahla and I went to the RAE Lounge in downtown Atlanta. It was a trendy lounge where many young professionals went to unwind. The RAE Lounge specializes in Caribbean food, poetry nights, hookahs, and happy hour.

I followed Nahla to a booth in the corner where a group was already sitting. I assumed that Nahla knew them. She sassed her way over and sat down.

"Hey, guys, this is my best friend, Trinity. Trinity, this is Corey, Jason, Kelly, and Brittany," Nahla said as she pointed to each one.

In unison, the group responded as they greeted me.

"Hey girl, come have a seat," the guy in black leggings with a shiny silver shirt motioned. His hair was pixie cut with blonde streaks. His face was beaten to the gods, hunty. I needed to take a lesson from him. His name was Corey.

As I was sitting down, the waitress came over to take our order. I glanced over the menu while everyone gave the waitress their order. I tried the lemon pepper wings and an apple martini.

"So, Trinity, what made you move to Atlanta?" Brittany asked.

Brittany's skin was butter pecan brown. Her black, curly hair came down to her shoulder. She had a very slender frame— she could be a model. She wore a blue mini dress with black 6-inch heels.

"Really, Brit? The girl just sat down, and you are already giving her the 3rd degree. It's none of your business", Kelly said as she sipped her martini.

Kelly was a petite figure with just the right amount of curves in all the right places. Her wavy hair fell to the middle of her back. She wore skinny jeans, a white blouse, and a black jacket. Cameron chimes in behind Kelly, "Yes, Brit, calm down. Let the child breathe; you are so noisy", snapping his fingers and bobbing his head.

"It's cool, I wanted a change," I answered.

Jason did not say much because he was more interested in his phone than the atmosphere. Jason was fair-skinned, with muscle tone, blonde hair, and blue eyes. However, he would only look up when a pair of lovely legs walked by. Just then, the waitress brought over our food and drinks just as Brittany was about to ask more questions. I swear she has got to be the most curious person or just plain noisy.

As the night went on, I started to enjoy myself. Cameron and I went to the dance floor together. That boy sure knows how to drop it low. I might have to have him teach me a couple of moves.

As we returned to the table after our fourth time on the dance floor, a tall, light-skinned man, medium with built muscle tone, caught my eye. He was different from the clean-cut guys I am used to dating. As our eyes locked for a second time, he finally decided to walk over to where Cameron and I were.

"Excuse me, Miss, do you have a moment?" How does he know if Cameron is my man or not?

"Um, yes," I said as he grabbed my hand and kissed it. I was perplexed, and I knew that my face probably showed it.

People have told me that my face always shows what I think, so I got to work on it.

"My name is Michael. What's yours?" he said while holding my hand.

"Trinity. Nice to meet you, Michael." I felt a little awkward from all the handholding. I guess he could tell because he finally let my hand go. Then, he offers to buy me a drink. So, we walked over to the bar and placed our order. For the rest of the night, Michael and I sat in the corner, away from everyone, and talked until it was almost closing time.

"Can I see you again?" Michael asked me.

"Sure, here is my number," I wrote down on a napkin at the club. Yeah, I said the reason for the move was to focus on me. After exchanging numbers, I met with Nahla, and we left.

On the drive home, the evening Michael and I spent together played repeatedly in my mind. His smile was so bright it could light up a room, and his cologne smelled so good. If this is a sign of what Atlanta offers, I am game.

New Town, Fresh Start

As I slowly opened my eyes, I could hear the chatter of the neighborhood kids outside waiting for their school bus and the sunlight streaming through the window blinds. As I lay on my king-size bed, reminiscing about my first night in Atlanta, the daydreaming was short-lived when I was startled by my alarm. I flung my hand wildly all over the nightstand until I could turn the alarm off. I lay down for a few more minutes before dragging myself out of bed.

"Good morning, sleepyhead," Nahla said with a smile as I zombie walked toward the bathroom.

Nahla is already dressed in a white button-down blouse, black pencil shirt, and 4-inch heels. She sat at the dining room table, sipping her tea and eating a bagel.

"Morning, Nahla," I muffle as I rub my eyes. I wondered how Nahla could still wake up and be so perky after a long night of partying. The thought crossed my mind, but I didn't bother to ask her. Instead, I mustered up enough energy to make it into the bathroom to take a shower and get ready for work.

On my first day at work, I decided to keep it simple. So, I wore a slick ponytail with a bun and a natural beat to the face. Since I was tired, I decided to dress the part of an accountant. So, I will stick with the basics: a two-piece black suit with a white blouse and some black pumps. Then, I glanced in the mirror to ensure everything was good; I headed toward the kitchen to make a coffee and grab a muffin.

"So, Trinity, are you going to give me the 411 on your new boo? What did you guys talk about, and will you see him again?" Nahla asks with a smirk on her face.

With a look of annoyance on my face, I grabbed my cup of coffee and headed toward the door.

"Bye, Nahla, let's be clear. He is not my NEW Boo, and there is nothing to discuss regarding Michael," I replied as I closed the door.

I could not close the door quickly enough; Nahla moaned, "Ooh, Michael is his name." I kept going toward my car as if I did not hear her.

As I was getting into my car, my phone rang. What now, Nahla, I thought to myself.

"Hello, Trinity?" a deep voice on the other end of the phone.

"Yes, this is Trinity. May I ask who is calling?" I replied.

"Good morning, sexy. This is Michael from last night, or did you forget me already?"

It would have been impossible for me to do so, but I did not want Michael to know I thought about him or hear the excitement in my voice about him calling.

Keeping calm, I kept telling myself, "How are you? What did I do to get an early morning call?"

"Well, you told me you started your new job today. So, I just wanted to make sure I am the first to tell you to have a good day on your first day of work and ask if you want to hang out with me and some friends?" Michael replied.

"Well, thank you for calling me. Unfortunately, I have to decline since this is my 1st week at work. I'm sorry.

"That's cool. I will call you later. Have a good day," Michael said, and then we hung up.

As I pull up to the parking gate outside my work building, a young man steps out from the security building in front of the parking garage.

"Good morning, Ms. Jones," the building security officer said as he handed me my parking placard.

He was decent-looking and looked to be in his early twenties.

With a confused look, I said, "Good Morning. Have I met you before?" The security guy just smiled, "No, ma'am. I have your ID badge here with your picture and car information. Because of security risks, we must run a background check on everyone before entering the building. Towne & Association Financial Group is located on the third floor. So here you go, and good luck on your first day." Then he handed me my access badge and parking placard

"Thank you, Sir," I replied, and then I drove into the parking garage and parked my car. I was so nervous but excited when I arrived at the office. I have always been interested in finance and was eager to start in my new role.

The elevator doors open on the third floor to a panoramic view of downtown Atlanta in the receptionist's background area. A young woman who looked to be in her early twenties sat at the reception desk. She was of slender build and dark hair; she was tough to miss. Her outfit was very revealing. I walked over to the desk where the young lady was sitting. "Good morning, my name is Trinity Jones. I am here to see Mr. Bell."

The receptionist told me to take a seat without looking up and that she would let Mr. Bell know. I could not believe what just happened. The receptionist was unprofessional and had no manners, let alone working at a Fortune 500 company. I politely turned around to walk over to the oak wood chair next to the elevator and sat down.

"Ah, good morning, Trinity. It's a pleasure to put a face with the name," Mr. Bell said as he headed toward me and shook my hand.

Mr. Bell was a short guy with brown eyes and a receding hairline. When I saw him, George Jefferson from the TV show The Jeffersons was the first person that came to mind. It was an early 1970s show my aunt used to watch.

"Good morning, Mr. Bell. I am so excited to get started," I exclaimed.

"That's great! Let me show you to your office. And I see that you have met my daughter, Jennifer," Mr. Bell said as he turned to walk down the hall.

That explains everything, I thought to myself as I followed Mr. Bell. She is the daughter of the boss.

Mr. Bell showed me around the office, introducing me to different departments and people. My coworkers were friendly and welcoming, as they greeted me. The fast-paced and professional atmosphere of the firm struck me.

We went into my new office to get an overview of the company. He was a seasoned financial expert, and I was intimidated by his wealth of knowledge and experience. But as we talked, I quickly realized he was approachable and supportive, which made me feel at ease.

"Here we are, Trinity. This is your office. Go ahead and get settled. If you need anything, Jennifer will assist you. Today, you have orientation and a meeting to help get you up to speed," Mr. Bell said as he walked out of my office.

I sat at my oak wood desk and admired the scenery from my large glass window overlooking the downtown. This view and office are breathtaking; a girl can get used to this. However, even the view could not get my mind off of Michael.

Michael will have to wait because I have to prepare my mind for the meeting and all my store training. My afternoon was occupied with orientation and meetings with various departments. I learned much about the company and its culture and was impressed by my coworkers' expertise and professionalism.

I was exhausted but exhilarated at the end of the day. I am so proud of myself for starting this new chapter in my career and was excited to continue learning and growing at the financial firm.

As I left the office, I couldn't help but smile. I was grateful for this opportunity and looked forward to my future at the company.

As the weekend came and I officially made it through my first week of work, I could not have been more thrilled to spend time with Michael. It was our second p date, so this time, it will be a little more intimate and relaxed at his house. He has planned a dinner and a movie, so I figure my black leggings and a T-shirt with some Uggs would be great. I grabbed my keys and phone and headed toward the door.

"So should I stay up or not," Nahla said with sarcasm as she stood in the hallway in her pink pajamas, short set, and black hair bonnet.

I glanced at her for a few seconds with my lips puckered up, and then I turned my head and walked toward the door.

"Nahla, I will be back. But you might not want to stay up," I said as I walked out the front door.

When I arrived at Michael's apartment, he was still cooking. I could tell that he was a little overwhelmed, but he tried to play it cool. Men, they never want you to know that they need help. He rushed back into the kitchen to continue chopping vegetables while his meat was searing, and some sauce simmered. So, I headed over to the sofa and sat down. His apartment décor was that of an actual bachelor pad. He had the primary, and none of the furniture matched. I hesitated to say anything because I did not want him to lose focus, so I sat back and observed him while he worked. Michael was wearing a pair of gray sweatpants and a white T-shirt. Unfortunately, but great for me, they left nothing to the imagination. He was even sexier than I remembered, and I was impressed by his effort to prepare dinner.

Once dinner was ready, we sat at the table and talked. The conversation was vague, now come to think of it. We talked about being from Florida, and you know, the usual things when you are trying to get to know someone. I must admit, the food was alright. Once we finished, we made our way to the sofa. We were about twenty minutes into the movies until we were quickly interrupted by the loud banging on his apartment door. I cannot believe this fool looked at me as if I had any idea who was at the door. So, I returned the look like isn't' this your house?

"Michael, who is that?" I said as I looked up at him.

"I don't know, stay here," he said as he got up to check. He returned in less than half of a second. "It's my baby mama. Shhhhh, do not say anything, and she will leave."

Was this happening? I could not believe I might have to retreat to my high school days. I needed to prepare myself to fight. Let's be clear: I DO NOT, and I will never fight over a guy. When I fight, it is only for self-defense.

"Michael, Michael! I know that you are in there. Open this damn door right now!" The female voice said on the other side of the door.

"And when do you think she will be leaving?" I asked. I looked at him like he was stupid while rushing to get together. What black woman you know just leaves, especially when she sees your car in the yard?

He replied with a nervous look, "She will." I gave Michael a look that if looks could kill, Michael would be lying on the floor.

"Michael, if you don't open this damn door. I will bust every window in this apartment," his baby mama said from the other side of the door. Before he could say anything, she was climbing through the window. Yes, like a damn monkey. I could not make this mess up. I was shaking my head in disbelief because I could not believe what I witnessed. The girl was halfway through the window when she started fussing and cussing at me.

"Calm down, Tanya," Michael said. So that's her name. I thought her name would have been something more ratchet than Tanya. I will admit I prejudged her actions and how she looked. She had two different neon colors in her hair. She wore booty shorts, which showed the unflattering of her thighs rubbing together. I got to give it to her because she has a lot of confidence, maybe too much.

"Michael, who in the hell is this?" as she pointed in my direction. "You got your child and me outside for her?" as she rolled her neck back and forth.

I looked and rolled my eyes upwards as though looking for answers from above, and her teeth clenched around her bottom lip.

"Look, I will let you handle this without me," I responded and headed for the door.

"Yeah, get the hell out," she said while Michael was holding her back.

I turned around with a sarcastic smile and nodded as if okay before walking out the door. As I went to step out of the door, I almost tripped over a pink car seat. I noticed Michael's daughter sleeping in it, so I grabbed the car seat to bring the baby inside. When I entered the apartment, Tanya came over and snatched the car seat from her. Unbothered by it, I left and got into her car.

As I drove home, I replayed what happened in my head. I thought I left this drama back in Florida. I could not wait to tell Nahla about this. Knowing her, she would want to return to fight the girl. This pattern has to stop, and I don't understand how and why I keep attracting the same type of guys. Yes, I am having a whole conversation with myself. Don't act like you don't do it.

Once I made it home, I noticed someone keyed my car from the front to the back of the vehicle on the passenger side. Now I am furious. With no hesitation, I called Michael. I explained to him what Tanya had done and that they needed to reimburse me. I did not wait for a response or anything as I hung up and proceeded into my apartment. To my relief, Nahla was already asleep. I did not want to relive the foolishness all in one night. Since I was not tired, I just sat on the sofa in the dark and quietness of my apartment to reevaluate things.

The whole purpose of my moving here was to do something different. I don't want to repeat what I was trying to leave. The more I thought about it, the more I realized that the problem might be me. But how and why is what I keep asking myself. I respect my elders, attend church, and help others when possible. And amid my thinking, I could hear my auntie quoting Psalm 37:4, "Baby, delight yourself in the LORD, and he will give you the desires of your heart. Trinity, when you truly rejoice in God's eternal things, your desires will begin to parallel His, and you will never go unfulfilled." Her purpose in saying that was to try to prevent me from moving. No matter where I go, it will not fulfill me. Well, that will stop TODAY!

Several weeks passed, and I still was waiting to hear from Michael, nor did he give me any money for my car. After that fiasco, I attended a church that was not far from my house. It was a massive church with over a thousand members; I was not used to that, but it felt like home. I finally had a sense of peace and clarity. Nahla even attended services with me.

Chapter Three

A FAMILIAR PATTERN

Chapter Three
A FAMILIAR PATTERN

Nahla and I decided to have a girl's night out to relieve a little stress from the work week, so we went to Miami Nights, a club on the Northwest side of Atlanta. Just because I decided to join the church did not make me a saint. I am still a work in progress.

I told Nahla I needed this because work has been so crazy. I had deadline after deadline and was still waiting for an end in sight. Nahla shook her head in agreement while putting on her makeup. The traffic on I-285 was light until we got to the club's parking lot. Then, the line to get into the club was long.

"Nahla, I think we will have to wait a while to get in. We will be lucky to get in there before the ladies' free before 11 pm is over," I said with an uncertain look.

"Girl! Don't worry; I know the security guard at the door." Nahla responded.

After parking my car, I checked to ensure my makeup was on point before entering. "Trinity, hurry up before the club gets too crowded," she said excitedly, acting like it was not already crowded.

"Ok, ok, I'm coming."

As we walked past people standing in line, I noticed a few girls giving us a nasty stare. You know, the ones like, who do they think they are all that type of look. I think I overheard one of them say, "Who do they think they are," to one of their friends. I walked like I just won Miss America and tossed my hair.

As we entered the club, which was already pulsing with energy, the smell of Caribbean spices wafted through the air, and the sound of reggae and hip-hop music filled the room. We made our way through the crowded club and over to the bar. Nahla waved her hand in the air to get the bartender's attention. The bartender was curvaceous; she wore plain ripped jeans and a midriff black shirt, noting she had a clean, heart-shaped face with soft hazel eyes. Her black hair was in a sleek back ponytail. She stopped talking to a group of guys and headed over to us.

"Hey ladies, what can I get you," the bartender asked with a smile.

"I will take an Amaretto sour."

"And can I get a Long Island Iced Tea," Nahla replied. "Sure thing, ladies," the bartender answered. She walked away and prepared the drinks. While making our drink, she swayed her hips back and forth to the music.

The DJ was jamming. The entire club was on the dance floor.

"Here you go, that will be $12.50," the bartender said.

Nahla paid for both drinks and then we headed over to the VIP. It is never a dull moment with us. We danced for hours to the DJ's songs. As the night wore on, we hit the dance floor. We swayed and twirled to the beat of the music, getting lost in the rhythm, dancing with some friends, laughing and having a great time. I just felt a tap on my shoulder, so I turned around to see who it was. "Excuse me, miss, don't I know you?" the guy said.

This guy we tall, with broad shoulders and a muscular build. He had a chiseled jawline and sharp features, with a warm smile that lit up his face. His confidence and charisma naturally drew people to him. He had a deep, rich voice and a kind demeanor, making him easy to talk to and instantly likable. He had a contagious energy about him. However, I quickly changed my tone from being standoffish when I saw his friends standing beside him.

Then I remember, "Oh yeah, Vegas Night Club."

Nahla and I met a group of guys there about three months before this trip. This club was about 45 minutes away, and we decided to go. We wanted to try something new. I don't remember meeting him that night at Vegas Night Club, but it all came together when I saw one of his friends there.

"My name is Trevor, but my friend calls me Tre. Can I get you a drink?" Trevor asks with an enticing smile.

"No, thank you. I am driving tonight," I replied with a flirtatious smile.

Then I turned back around toward the dance floor and danced with Nahla. I did not return to the foundation for a minute when some annoying guy came behind me and started gyrating. I stopped dancing, turned around annoyedly, and walked off. As I walked through the crowd, another guy grabbed my hand and pulled me in his direction. I snatched my hand from the man and walked over to where Trevor and his friends were.

This guy kept pulling my arm as Trevor was talking to me. "Act like you're my boyfriend," I whisper in Trevor's ear. The smile on Trevor's face told me he concurred.

At that point, I turn around and dance with Trevor. I could tell he seemed slightly confused or maybe timid initially, but then he relaxed and wrapped his arms around my waist. He loosened up more once the DJ played reggae. For the rest of the night, Trevor and I were inseparable. Until Nahla came up to let me know it was time to go. Nahla was exhausted, but I was still buzzing with energy. Apprehensively, I nodded my head to Nahla and then whispered bye in Trevor's ear.

As we approached the exit, Trevor ran behind me and grabbed my hand.

"Can I get your number?" he asked. I nodded, put my number in his phone, and left the club.

Nahla and I chatted about our night on the drive home and how aggressive the men were at the club, but we could not wait to get in our beds. I did not get my hopes up about speaking to Trevor anytime soon or ever. However, I enjoyed dancing with him and hanging out with his friends.

Despite hanging out late last night, we still got up in time to go to church. I heard the choir from the parking lot singing an uplifting old-school hymn. After the choir sang two songs, the congregation converged to the pulpit as the preacher stood up and spoke. When this man of God started preaching, I felt uneasy and started looking around me. I thought the pastor was speaking directly to me. Looking down as if I could give myself a quick glimpse, do I still look like last night's party girl or a Jezebel? Was this a sign from God? I will avoid all eye contact until I get out of here.

Bishop Thomas preaches from Proverbs 3:5-6. And once I heard the scripture, I knew this was my affirmation to strengthen my relationship with God. It was time I trusted in Him rather than my understanding and wisdom. In doing so, He will help me not misinterpret His messages.

His voice filled the room with authority and conviction. His words were powerful, and he spoke with as contagious passion and enthusiasm hanging on every word and nodding in agreement.

Although this was not the first time, I heard it. As a child, my aunt, who was adamant about attending church, read the bible daily. She would talk about Proverbs 3:5-6 but pressed that scripture when I left for college. It took going through a failed engagement, a baby-mama altercation, and relocation to finally get what my auntie was trying to tell me. I could have avoided this if I had listened earlier in life, instead of doing things *my* way. The music snapped me out of my train of thought. With tears, I rose to my feet and praised the Lord. That Sunday, I left the church with a new outlook. Nahla and I spent the rest of the day at home, relaxing and preparing for the rest of the week.

After having two affirmations, I officially committed to God. Despite the devil trying to test me, I remained focused over the next several months, and my time consisted of going to work, school, and church. To relieve stress, my bestie and I would go shopping. And we did a lot of shopping. I spent more time with my Georgia family, as well. My growth was satisfactory, and I even got a promotion at work. I have been going about my usual routine for a few months now, trying to move on from the disappointment and emotional experience.

I was doing great at work, making new friends, and slowly finding my footing in Atlanta. One Saturday night, my phone rang while Nahla and I sat comfortably on the couch while watching a movie with Nahla. It was an unfamiliar number with a 401-area code. I would not answer it, but Nahla became annoyed after the third call and insisted. So, I answered it, not recognizing the number, and was immediately shocked to hear the voice on the other end.

"Hi, Trinity. This is Trevor. I wanted to see if you wanted to hang out with me, " Trevor said.

"Oh hey, Trevor. No, not tonight. I have bills and must go to work tomorrow," I replied.

"Okay. Well, can I come over after I leave the club," asked Trevor.

"Sure, call me when you are on your way," I said, then hung up the phone.

My opinion instantly changed about Trevor. I could not believe he thought coming over here so late was appropriate.

"He must be trippin. I am no one's booty call," I told Nahla. Nahla's eyes were glued to the television screen. I don't think she even noticed when I got up to get a drink.

As we were about to go to bed, there was a knock on the door. I knew it was not Trevor because I never gave him my address. Nahla and her boyfriend were going through it, so it could not have been him. We looked at each other, confused. Finally, I nonverbally decided to go and see who it was. I opened the door, and to my surprise, it was Michael. When Nahla saw who it was, she shook her head and walked toward her bedroom.

The look on my face was a dead giveaway as to what I was thinking. I had been waiting to hear from Michael for over four months when I asked him to fix my car. Although I was mad and confused about his presence at my doorstep, I was excited to see him in some strange, twisted way. I would be fighting a losing battle if I let him in.

"Hey, baby, I miss you. Can we talk"?

"Sure, come in." Before we could even take a step into my room, Michael grabbed me and tried to kiss me, but I pushed him away. Regaining my composure, "What makes you think you can come over here unannounced, with no apology or money to fix my car that your baby mama scratched?"

"What, um. I have been meaning to call you." Michael responded in surprise.

"Save it. You can't even get your lie straight," I said with my arms folded as I stared at Michael. If looks could kill, he would be dead. Michael sat on the bed with a nonchalance look before giving his excuse.

"Man, Trinity, it's not like that. I had so much going on. I miss you," Michael replied. Just then, my phone rang. I looked over at the nightstand and noticed Trevor calling. I did not want to add more drama, so I sent him to voicemail after the third call.

"Who is that? Your other nigga?" Michael asked.

Standing with my hands on my hips, I told him it was none of his business and asked him to leave. Surprised by my actions, he gathered himself and walked to the door. He muffled how I would regret it, but I brushed it off my shoulder and slammed the door. As I sat on my bed, Trevor called three more times that night, but I was not in the mood, so I turned my phone off and went to sleep.

Usually, I am off on the weekend, but the company had a significant project deadline, so it was a mandatory workday for everyone. I got up out of my bed and jumped in the shower. I turned on the radio and listened to some music and recapped what happened in the world last night. How could Michael be mad, I wonder? And who in the hell did Trevor think I was, calling me at midnight? Why in the world do I keep attracting these good-for-nothing guys? I reach to turn the shower off and grab my fluffy white towel.

While putting on my clothes, I noticed the blinking light on my cell phone, so I reached over and played the voicemail. It was several messages from Trevor. The messages said he was on his way but needed my address and to call him back. The other three messages noted that he just got off on my exit. I shook my head in disbelief as I threw my phone into my purse and headed to the kitchen for a coffee cup.

To my surprise, Nahla's secret boyfriend, John, was making himself at home in the fridge. I do not understand what Nahla sees in him. He only comes around for the nightly booty call and then is out.

"Hey, Trinity, what's up?" John said.

"Good morning, John. Um, where is Nahla?" I asked with a disturbed expression as I glanced around, looking for Nahla.

"Oh, she is in the room getting ready," John responded. Once I made my cappuccino, I dashed out the door without saying bye. Tonight, Nahla and I needed to confer on our third leaching roommate.

As I was about to walk into my office, I ran into Giselle. She was one of my coworkers who helped train me. Giselle was of Louisiana Creole origin and was in her early twenties. You could hear her New Orleans accent when she talked. Giselle wore her jet-black hair straight, which complemented her cinnamon skin hue. Her petite frame made everything she wore look good.

"Ms. Giselle, how was your weekend?" I ask with excitement in my tone.

"What's good, T. It was okay. I can't complain," Giselle replied.

Giselle's tomboyish way did not fit her appearance, but I loved hanging with her. I appreciate that Giselle would be straightforward, no matter what. I walked into my office, sat down, and grabbed my notebook for the company meeting. As we made our way to the elevator, I caught Giselle up with all the shenanigans of "As Trinity Turns." As I was telling her, I could not help but notice the look on her face. First, her eyes widened, and then her mouth dropped. I could tell that she was shocked.

"Trinity, finish telling me the story right after the meeting. Girl, you are a mess," Giselle said as she entered the conference room.

I shook my head and followed behind her. I did not have a response because it was true. I felt embarrassed by her comment, although she was honest. Why does she have to be honest all the damn time? Ugh, that darn, Giselle. She knew how to get me to overthink things. I kept thinking about her comment. I was still trying to figure out what the meeting was about.

Instead of going out for lunch, we ordered in and ate in my office to complete our chat about the weekend.

"See, if you would have given my brother some love, maybe you all would still be together," Giselle said with a grin.

"Well, he still has some maturing to do. You and your mom still baby this twenty-five-year-old man," I responded as I scrunched my nose and curled my mouth.

"Girl, you are silly, but fault my mama for that," Giselle reclined in the chair and laughed.

Jennifer said," Um, Trinity, you have a phone call on line one."

Giselle whispered as she echoed Jennifer's words. I shook my head because her imitation of Jennifer was on point.

"Thank you, Jennifer. Send the call through."

As I picked up the call, Giselle got up and waved bye to head into her office.

"Hello, this is Trinity Smith. How may I help you?"

"Hi, Ms. Smith; what do I have to do to get a woman like you out on a date without being stood up?" the voice on the other end of the phone asked.

"Excuse me? Who is this? I do not have time for games. I can play games with my little brother if I want to play them. Who is this?" I responded in a harsh tone.

"Calm down, Trinity. This is Trevor. Sorry, I was just fooling around," Trevor replied. Unsure of what he called for; I remained on the phone to entertain him for a little.

"So, when you get off, can we go out?" Trevor suggested.

"Sure," I replied, tapping my pen on my desktop.

"Bet, but can I get your address this time before you go? I don't want last night to repeat itself," Trevor stated. I must admit that I was a little curious about what Trevor meant by that, but I brushed it off and gave him my address.

As I was hanging up, Giselle peeped back into my office to mention Mr. Bell's conference. I wondered if this girl had a tracker or camera in my office.

"Hey, sis, so which one is that?" Giselle said with a sneer on her face and waggled her trim eyebrows.

I stared at her and shook my head as I picked up the files and cell phone. "Let's go crazy, lady, and go to this meeting," I said as I passed Giselle at the door. Giselle followed behind as we made our way to Mr. Bell's office.

"Oh. I understand why they are going after you, sis, all that ass," Giselle said with amusement. I look back over my shoulder at her with my nose wrinkled up.

After the meeting, I left work early. It gave me time to run some errands and get a manicure and pedicure before my date with Trevor. As I was getting dressed, there was a knock on the door. I glanced at the clock on the wall and noticed Trevor was on time.

"Give me a few minutes. I am almost ready," I said as I opened the door and let Trevor in. He stared at me for what seemed like an eternity. Did I have something on my face or something? It was a little awkward at first, but for some strange reason, I found it flattering. I noticed he was eyeing my body. His look showed that this date would be like all the others. Why do guys constantly undress women before they get to know us? I brush it off, "Give me 10 minutes, and I will be ready." I head to my room to finish getting dressed.

After a few minutes, I reemerge with my Chloe purse on my shoulder and shades on my head. "So, do you want to tell me what you meant by not wanting to repeat the other night?" Although I knew what he meant by it, I wanted to hear his answer.

"Well, when I left the club the other night, I called you several times, but you did not answer. You were okay with it when I asked about coming over before I left. Although you didn't answer, I still drove this way, but all I knew was that you lived on Cascade Road. So, I tried calling you once I made it to the exit. Unfortunately, you never picked up the phone. I stay 45 minutes away from you, and I was too drunk to drive back. So, I slept in my car on I-285", he explained.

"What in the world made you do that? I'm sorry, my phone was on vibrate all night," as my eyebrows raised and curved.

I glanced in the mirror and turned to Trevor, "Again, I am sorry."

"Where are we going?" I asked as we got into his truck.

"Isn't there a mall close by," he inquired.

"Yeah, Greenbrier Mall is not too far from here," I replied. I prefer Lenox or Cumberland Mall, though. Greenbrier does not have much to offer store-wise, and the environment reminds me too much of home. Greenbrier is somewhere I would go in high school, not now.

Despite my opinion about the mall, that's where he wanted to go. Although I did not want to go, my opinion did not matter. So, while en route to the mall, we chatted about our childhood a little and realized we had many things in common. The more we talked, the more comfortable we became with one another. However, I was suspicious about this unorthodox date of going to the mall. It did not help matters when Trevor asked my opinion on picking out shoes for himself. Not once did he ask if I wanted a drink or a pretzel. I am used to being wined and dined; what am I doing here? I had to continue convincing myself that I needed to try something different because the familiar things had just reached a dead end. We spent the next few hours browsing the stores and trying various outfits. We laughed and joked together and continued to talk about our interests, family, and future. I felt a strong connection with Trevor and was grateful for the opportunity to get to know him better.

After Trevor finished shopping for some shoes, we headed toward his truck. For some odd reason, Trevor trails behind me. Even though he tried to play it off as if he was admiring my body, it was a complete failure. Trevor reached for his phone and recorded me walking. From his phone conversation, I could tell that he forwarded it to his buddy. I fully knew of it but just played it off. I see he still had a little growing up to do.

As we got off the exit for my apartment, we noticed an African art festival going on, so we decided to stop and check it out. Walking through the festival and smelling all that food made me so hungry. My stomach rumbled, but the loud music drowned it out. I anticipated that Trevor would offer to get me something to eat. I tried to give him hints, but he did not get it.

Ugh, men can be so naïve sometimes. We continued wandering through all the vendors' tents until we arrived upon one with many portraits. As I discussed the different pictures, Trevor's eyebrows flew up in astonishment. I suppose he thought I was all looks. He purchased two items, but none of them were food. Finally, we headed back to my apartment to chill.

The ride was about 10 minutes. When we got home, I decided to cook a good old Southern meal since I was not offered a meal on this date. Although I should have sat before Trevor and eaten my food, I even asked him if he wanted something. Trevor gave me the same look he gave me at the art festival. Where did this guy come from, the woods or something? He acted as if he had never seen a pretty woman who was smart and could cook. Yes, I am a triple threat. What can I say? My aunt raised me well.

So, I made him a plate. We decided to watch television since Nahla was not coming home until late. Our conversation was so different from the other guys I dated. I felt so relaxed with him; it was as if I had known him for years. We eventually dozed off but were quickly awakened by a car alarm outside. Thinking he was slick, Trevor asked if he could stay the night. Although I realized what he was trying to do, I said okay. My brain was telling me, *Trinity- tell him NO!*

We made our way into my bedroom, but before I got into bed, I put on a pair of sweatpants to go to bed. I did not want Trevor to get any ideas.

"Can I hold you," Trevor asked.

"Sure, but do not get any ideas," I replied in a low-voiced.

As I lay back toward Trevor, he grabs me by my waist pulls me closer. I could feel him breathing on the back of my collar. He rubs his hand down the side of my hips and onto my legs. Without losing a beat, he kissed the back of my neck. I quickly realized what he was thinking, and it would not take place. What type of woman did he assume I was to have sex on the first date? Hell, he did not even get me a drink on whatever you call a date. I drag his hand back up and turn on my belly.

"Go to sleep, Trevor."

"Can I make love to you," he whispers.

"Boy, you don't even know me." Thinking to myself, that must be the lamest line ever!

I look over at him with my face frowned up. "No, you can go to sleep or home. I do not get down like that."

Trevor rolled over, in dissatisfaction, and went to sleep. I was unsympathetic and went to sleep.

"Good night," I smirked. But Trevor did not respond.

As dawn approached, we woke back up to the sound of tapping on my bedroom door.

"T, are you going to church today? If so, you need to get up and get dressed," Nahla said from the other side of the door.

"Yes, Nahla. I'm getting up now," I replied.

I rose out of my bed and grabbed my robe. As I glanced through my wardrobe for something to wear, Trevor started to get dressed. I could see he wished to sleep in a little longer. So, I grabbed my purple wrap dress and black strap heels and headed to the bathroom to shower. Once I returned from the restroom, Trevor sat on the corner of my bed, staring into his phone.

I enjoyed my time with Trevor and looked forward to our next date. I felt comfortable and at ease with him and was excited to see where this could go.

"So, what now?" I inquired.

"What do you mean?" as he gazes up from his cell phone.

"Where do we go from here? Or are you going to play games because I would not have sex with you?"

"No, Trinity. I like you. Let's see where things will go. Is that okay with you? Or are you done?" Trevor said with a grin.

"You are full of jokes this morning. Well, when will I see you?"

"How about you call me after you get out of church? And then I will come back over," Trevor said before embracing and kissing me on the lip.

I assume he was surprised I went to church. Don't judge me. We all are human and give in to weakness; the only difference is that I admit mine. We all walked to the automobiles and said our goodbyes before entering them.

Nahla and I made it in time to perform our church duties. Nahla was part of the church choir, and I joined the hospitality group. My obligations were to acknowledge people as they came into the church and aid them if they needed help. This duty was my initial stride in becoming closer to the Lord. Our worship service always opened with the choir singing praises, followed by honor and devotion to glorify God by concentrating on him. That morning, the choir had the roof rocking off the church. The pastor's sermon of the day concentrated on inspiring the congregation. He focused on advancing the congregation's faith into movement. The interpretations he gave pulled on my spirit and pushed me to action.

Most Sundays after church, Nahla and I chilled at home in our pajamas, relaxing before the workweek. I made supper, as I always did. Nahla disliked cooking, to be honest, and I was unsure if she even knew how to cook. As the meal was cooking, I called Trevor to tell him I was back home. I could not wait to see him again.

"So, you are just going to walk by me and not explain what transpired between you and Trevor," Nahla said with a devilish smirk.

"Nahla, you are a mess. Tre is a nice guy. We talked all night about our family and expectations."

"Dang T, you'll go on one date, and you are already talking about marriage," Nahla replied. Whenever Nahla calls me T, she is serious.

"Girl, calm your spirits. Ain't nobody talking about marriage or rushing. We are taking things slow and steady. Plus, I'm unsure about him and moving forward with a relationship."

With her inward slanting eyebrows and lips pressed, "Why? Does he have a crazy baby mama? He probably lives with his mom or is married. It sounds too good to be true."

"No, Nahla, none of the above. He is a contractor for the government. After dealing with Jarvis and your brother, I am cautious. I do not want to take part in the hassles and emotional bull crap." I came back with my eyes fixed on the television screen.

Jarvis and Nahla's brother cheated on me and married the other woman. Nahla's brother also told my college roommate that he was ending our relationship before he told me. Then he called me to acknowledge his mistake and apologize. While getting the third degree from Nahla, Trevor texted me to let me know he could not make it due to work.

Nahla knew from my comment that I did not want to talk about it anymore, so we continued to watch the new season of *The Housewives*. It was growing late when the series went off, so I went to bed. I had a long day ahead and needed my rest. I waved goodnight to Nahla, and I went to my room. The phone rang just as I laid my head on my pillow.

Even though Trevor couldn't join us tonight, I was ecstatic to hear his voice. Our conversation lasted for hours, and it genuinely felt like we had known each other for ages. Our childhood experiences were remarkably alike.

"How was church? Did you enjoy it"?

"Yes, it was great. Maybe next time you can go."

"Sure, we can go next Sunday. I will spend the weekend at your place."

"That will be great, babe, and yes, I will be there when I get off. Just make sure you text me when you make it home."

As we said our goodbyes and hung up the phone, a sense of joy overwhelmed me, and I retired to bed with a beaming smile. I felt like a teenage girl experiencing her first crush at that moment. I wondered whether or not he might be "the one." What would our potential children look like, and does he even envision having children? These musings about our future captivated my mind until I drifted into slumber.

Chapter Four

THE UNEXPECTED

Chapter Four
THE UNEXPECTED

Things have been going wonderfully between Trevor and I over the past five and a half months. I was thrilled to have received a promotion last week. Trevor was eager to take me out to celebrate, but unfortunately, I had to postpone our plans.

Feeling exhausted and irritable, I decided to stay in and spend a cozy evening with Trevor. As I prepared for his arrival, I took a relaxing shower and settled in. It was then that I noticed the calendar on my wall, and I couldn't help but feel a rush of concern when I realized I was three weeks late for my menstrual cycle. I chose to wait to raise the issue with Trevor until I had confirmed the situation.

I dashed to the bathroom, frantically rummaging under the bathroom sink for my stash of pregnancy tests. I understood it might seem excessive, but I preferred to prepare for unexpected situations. After taking the test, I perched on the toilet, anxiously awaiting the results. Those five minutes felt like an eternity, my mind swirling with countless thoughts. From the very start of our relationship, we had never used protection, and the topic of children hadn't crossed our minds. Our relationship was still in its blooming stage. Glancing at the result on the bathroom sink, the word "pregnant" became apparent on the test screen.

I lingered in the restroom for another ten minutes, the passing time seemingly stretching into eternity before I summoned the courage to step into the shower. My thoughts raced at a frenetic pace. After mustering up my nerves, I resolved to be candid with Trevor and share my feelings. Approximately 40 minutes later, a knock echoed through the door. Taking a deep breath, I sighed and finally opened it.

Before Trevor entered, he leaned in and kissed my cheek warmly. His perplexed expression indicated his confusion over my prolonged absence. Still reeling from the revelation, I felt the overwhelming urge to retreat and process everything. Nevertheless, I knew I had to converse with Trevor to ensure clarity and understanding in our relationship.

" We need to talk," I explained.

Trevor's expression changed in an instant. It was as if he had stepped on a nail, his eyes widening in shock. I knew there was no avoiding telling him, but I also knew it would be difficult for him to process.

"Well, there's no easy way to say this. So, I'm just going to say it. I'm pregnant," I said, my voice trembling as I locked eyes with him.

I studied his body language, trying to gauge his reaction. The room fell utterly silent; his silence was deafening. The weight of the quiet filled the air, making it feel like an eternity.

"Did you hear me? Hello?" I asked.

"Yes, I heard you. What do you want to do?" Trevor responded.

"By 'you,' do you mean what we will do? This situation is about both of us, not just me. And I'm determined to keep it," I said, my voice steady and persistent, radiating my unwavering determination.

Trevor rose from his seat and strode toward the window. I strained to catch snippets of his murmurs about grappling with the difficult task of breaking the news to his mother. Although it struck a chord with me, I wanted to avoid pressing the issue. He needed time to understand the situation, so I retreated to my room to collect my thoughts.

A few minutes later, Trevor entered the room and sat beside me. He touched my stomach and spoke softly, "No matter what you decide, I'll be right by your side. We'll navigate through this together. I love you." A sense of tranquility washed over me with his head resting against my chest. For a moment, I had feared I might tread the same path as my mother and become a single parent. His words reassured me that we would be okay. I tenderly stroked his head until we both drifted off to sleep.

Despite the early stage of my pregnancy, I decided to share the news with my auntie. Her reaction took me by surprise. Gone was the stern figure I had known; instead, genuine excitement and concern for my well-being was my auntie's reaction. Our phone conversation provided me with immense comfort. For the first time in years, I could openly confide in her in a heart-to-heart conversation between women.

Later that evening, Trevor and I savored a delightful dinner at my favorite restaurant before retiring to his place. He often took me to this spot after a misunderstanding or when he needed to make amends. We spent the hours conversing, discussing our day and our upcoming visit to his family.

As we left the restaurant, I started experiencing abdominal pain, which left me feeling weak and unable to walk. Trevor immediately helped me to the car, and we drove to the hospital. After waiting for three hours, the doctor informed me that I was in the early stages of a miscarriage. I was devastated and wondered if this was punishment for my past mistakes. The entire car ride to his house was silent, and I felt that Trevor didn't want to say the wrong thing, so he said nothing. Deep down, I thought he was happy about it, so there was no need to explain it to his mom.

Once we arrived at his house, I went upstairs to lie down. My emotions were everywhere, and I didn't want to deal with anyone, including his roommate's girlfriend. Trevor stayed downstairs with his roommate, while I rested. Two hours later, Trevor came up with a glass of water, and the doctor prescribed medication for my pain. I took the meds and went back to sleep.

The next day, I woke up to Trevor getting ready for work. The doctor suggested that I stay off from work for a couple of days to let the miscarriage take its course, so I planned just to relax and sleep through it.

"How are you feeling, babe?" Trevor asked as he put on his uniform.

"I'm still in pain and tired. I think I am just going to go home."

"Are you sure? You know you can stay here until I get off," he said.

"Yes, I am sure. I will call you later," I replied.

"Okay, I will come over when I get off," he said.

I nodded in agreement as we walked to our cars. I took a little longer because the pain had gotten worse, but I tried to play it off because I did not want Trevor to know. He would probably try to urge me to stay at his house. So, I strolled with a slight hunch and my arms on my belly, struggling not to let the pain show on my face. It felt like the car was parked several miles away. Ugh, I just need to get inside and sit down. I kept telling myself.

Once I made it home, I showered and went straight to bed. The following couple of days were a blur. I spent my days sleeping and only getting up to take a shower. Sorrow and pain are a combination that does not mix. Trevor had been so supportive through the whole ordeal. I think the loss of our child brought us closer together.

I returned to work after the miscarriage ran its course and took some extra vacation days. My outward appearance seemed like I had it all together, but I was a mess. My heart ached from losing my unborn baby. I could not help but question if I had done something wrong. The continual thoughts of what gender it was ran through my mind regularly. "Trinity, get it together," I whispered to myself. I have so much work to catch up on. I am so grateful that Giselle offered to help once she finished her two appointments. I do not think I would have made it through this week if it was not for her. Just as I was packing my things to leave, Jennifer buzzed in to tell me Trevor was on the phone.

"Hey, how are you?" Trevor asked.

"I'm okay, and you? "I asked.

"I could be better. I have something to tell you. My job is relocating me to Washington DC, but I want you to come with me," Trevor said.

I responded, "We already had this talk. I am not moving anywhere without a ring. If we broke up, I have to figure out what I would do."

"Before I go to Washington, DC, I have a six-month detailed assignment in Canada. So, I have a lot of stuff to take care of. I have to get all my legal stuff in order; we need to get married, and I have to pack," Trevor stated.

"Repeat that?"

"Repeat what, baby?" Trevor questioned.

"The married part. Are you asking me to marry you?"

"Yeah. Call the court to see what we need to do."

"Oh, okay. Are you sure?"

"Yes, I am sure," I assured him.

Despite having dated him for only eight months, I was surprisingly calm about marrying Trevor. It's a feeling that's hard to describe but felt right. Perhaps it's because I thought it was part of God's plan for me. My only concern was that he might not show up at the courthouse.

I excitedly phoned my aunt and uncle to share the news of my impending nuptials. As usual, my aunt took the news positively, but my uncle was upset that Trevor hadn't sought his permission to marry me. It's unreasonable, given that I haven't lived with them for five years. I'm sure he'll eventually come around and give us his blessing.

Over the next few weeks, Trevor and I traveled to the courthouse to exchange our vows and handled all the necessary legal and financial matters. We decided that I would continue living with Nahla until his return.

After weeks of planning, the big day was finally here. Today was like any other day, except I would become Mrs. Johnson by noon. I worked half a day and later met Trevor on his lunch break at the courthouse. There was nothing fancy about us. He had on his uniform, and I was business casual. Although it was just the judge and us, it still felt intimate and unique. I will admit that I was nervous about being his wife. Am I ready to be someone's wife? No more living a life of fun? Oh well, it's too late to back out now.

Once the ceremony was over, Trevor and I went to grab something to eat before returning to work. Then, I headed home to wait for my husband. I kept repeating the words repeatedly in my head: MY HUSBAND. I cannot believe I am someone's wife. Did I do this? I was still in shock but in a good way. I am finally a three-fold woman. Finally, I have found myself, my husband, and my Lord.

Trevor lived in the tranquil suburbs northwest of downtown Atlanta, a comfortable forty-five-minute drive from my location. Arriving at his workplace after work, I prepared a delightful dinner and set the scene for a romantic and serene evening. His roommate was out of town, so we had the house to ourselves.

As soon as my husband entered, we gratefully embraced, savoring the moment. When I led him to the dining room, his surprised expression was priceless. We shared a cozy meal, and later, we retired upstairs to Trevor's inviting bedroom. There was another surprise, so I let Trevor enter the room first. As he opened the door, the room held a dozen roses lit by scented candles.

"Wow, Babe, you went all out. Thank you, Mrs. Johnson," he said as he grabbed my hand and pulled me into the room.

"You're welcome, Mr. Johnson," I replied with a flirtatious grin.

Trevor grabbed me, pulled me towards him, and kissed me. His kisses were soft but intriguing. At this moment, I surrendered myself to him. As we kissed, we undressed each other until all our clothes were off. Although we have been here before, this time was different. He stared into my eyes before our lips locked again.

I found myself deeply moved at that moment. The unyielding intensity in Trevor's eyes spoke volumes about his sincere devotion to me. It's hard to put into words the overwhelming emotions I experienced. No wife can genuinely express her thoughts despite her husband's romantic desires. It's an indescribable sensation. The moment was truly sacred, brimming with sensuality, and it was nothing short of incredible as we merged and became one. It was a profoundly spiritual experience as if we had transcended a different realm. As the enthusiasm waned, the room gradually came back into focus. With one last sigh, Trevor collapsed beside me. I nestled in his arms, and together, we fell asleep, relishing the lingering essence of our intimate connection. I know it may sound cliché, but in that moment, the missing piece of my life's puzzle fell into place. Thank you, God.

I am seeing my husband off, having only been married for less than thirty days. We never spent a week apart, let alone six months, and on the other side of the world. I don't know what to do with myself while he is gone. We have been inseparable these past couple of months since we met. Trevor never made me doubt our relationship. He always made me feel like I was his everything. I could put my guard down with him, something I could never do with the men in my past. This man had broken entirely down my wall. I wanted to spend every moment with him. He is my best friend.

We spent our last weekend together in South Carolina before he had to check-in. On the ride there, we had some minor issues—or at least that is what I thought; maybe they predicted what would come. Don't worry; I will explain later.

We made it to our hotel room to freshen up before we headed to dinner. The mood was gloomy because we both were not ready for this separation. I hoped it would only make us stronger rather than grow apart. Trevor finally told me why he had not told his parents we were married. For some odd reason, his mom thinks I want his money and am a *wild one*. I hope that by sharing my experiences, you can empathize with the unfair judgment I face.

For one, I have had my share of NFL players, hip-hop artists, and several street pharmaceutical reps, all of whom made more money than her son in a month. But I chose not to be with them. And trust they are still calling for another chance. On top of calling me wild or out there, I can quote and apply the Bible like any other Christian. These "holier-than-thou small town church folks kill me. Judge not unless you want to be judged.

"Trinity! Trinity!" Trevor yelled.

The scream startled me from my train of thought. "Yes?" I responded.

"You, okay? I was asking what you wanted to eat."

"It doesn't matter."

"Okay, well, I am going to take a quick nap, and then we can eat."

As Trevor slept, I watched TV. Fifteen minutes later, Trevor's phone buzzed. I wanted to make sure it was not his mom, so I checked it. It was some strange number that texted him.

The message said, "Since I told you about me, how about you tell me a little about yourself."

Instead of waking him up, I called it back. The voice on the other end was female.

"Hello," the unfamiliar voice said.

"Hello, did you text Trevor?"

"Um, yeah, I met him last night. Who is this?"

"This is his wife. I see there is something he should have mentioned. Please make this the last time you contact him, and I'm about to let him know and inform him to do the same." Then I hung up the phone.

As I turn to look at this lying, unfaithful man, I try to make sure I do not lose control and murder him. The anger consumed me, and I threw his phone at his head. Trevor jumps up with a confused look on his face.

"So, you were supposed to have gone out with your boys to celebrate your leaving, but instead, you want to pick up females."

"Damn, that shit hurts. Trinity, what are you talking about? I did not holler at anybody."

"Now, you want to insult me. I already called the chick back, and she told me everything."

The dumb look on Trevor's face touches a nerve in my spine. I could feel my muscles tensing up. I paced back and forth in the hotel room, clinging my hand to my fist. I'm trying not to look at him because I would not be liable for my actions if I did.

"Calm down, Trinity. I let my boy hold my phone," he said, trying to soothe the situation, but my frustration was palpable as I paced the room.

"Oh, said the stupid ass story you will give me. So that's the game you want to play. Oh, okay, let the games begin. You have officially written a check your ass can't cash." I said, my voice filled with determination as I stormed out of the hotel room.

I had no clue where I was going since we were in South Carolina, and I left the car keys in the room. So, I went to the hotel bar and charged them in the room. It was not a cool two minutes before my cell phone rang. The call could change everything.

"What, Trevor!"

"Babe, can you please return to the room so we can talk? I will explain everything. I'm sorry."

"Yeah, bye," and I abruptly hung up the phone.

I decided to remain seated for ten minutes, contemplating the recent events, before contacting Giselle to recount what had transpired. Despite her desire to intervene, she managed to lift my spirits with her usual humor.

Upon returning to the room, I found Trevor fully dressed and perched on the edge of the bed, attempting to explain the situation. However, I remained unconvinced and promptly ended the conversation, making it clear that further transgressions would lead to considering divorce. We then went out to dinner.

We rose early to have breakfast the following day before seeing Trevor off. Despite lingering emotions from the previous night, I endeavored to set them aside and make the most of our remaining time together. Although our discussions centered mainly on his needs and business matters, Trevor noticed my efforts to be supportive.

As we made our way to the military base gate, my feelings changed from anger to sadness. I don't know how this guy can make me change my emotions so quickly. Any other guy, I would have been out in a heartbeat. But maybe because he isn't any other guy, he is my husband.

"ID, please," the guard at the gate asked sternly.

Snapping out of my trance, I reached into my purse and handed it to Trevor. So that he could give it to the guard. This is happening. After the guard cleared to pass, Trevor pulled up to check-in. While he unloaded, tears slowly flowed down my eyes. I did not want him to go. He was my best friend, my lover, my ace.

My bed would feel so large; now, he would not be there to hold me in his arms.

"Come on, Trinity, be strong for him," I thought as I tried to assure myself before Trevor returned. Watching Trevor return to the car, I quickly glance in the mirror to fix my face.

"Hey babe, I am all registered, so get out and let me rub my body one last time."

"Um, this body belongs to me, but you can have one more feel," I said as I exited the car.

"I love you and will call you when I settle in."

"Okay, love you. Bye, babe."

We kissed and hugged one last time before he left to walk into the office. The sounds of other families saying their goodbyes filled the air. Then, I got back in the car and watched my husband walk toward the door until I could not see him anymore, the familiar buildings of the base fading from view.

It felt like he was walking out of my world for good. A teardrop rolled down my face as I put the car in reverse. Once I made it off base, the tears ran like a stream. I could no longer keep it together. Just thinking about how we would be apart for the next six months or something happening to him made me cry uncontrollably. The overwhelming flood of emotions was too much to bear. Then, just as I was entering the highway, a recognizable voice called and said, "Hello?"

"Trevor?" I said as I choked back the tears, hoping that I could conceal my sadness.

"Yes, babe, why did it take you so long to leave?"

"How did you know that I didn't leave right away?" I asked in a high-pitched voice.

"I was looking out of the window. Stop crying. These few months will go by fast. I will call and email you every chance I get. I need you to be strong for us, okay?"

He always knows what to say to support me. With him as my cheering squad, I can do anything.

"I know, Tre, but it is just so hard. We spent every day together for the last couple of months, and now you are leaving. We have not been married long, only for thirty days."

"How about you plan a trip with the girls or a honeymoon spot for when I return?"

This man can be so thoughtful, putting me before himself. I should motivate and support him, but it's the reverse. We chatted for about another twenty minutes before we said goodbye.

Chapter Five

A MOTHER'S PAIN

Chapter Five
A MOTHER'S PAIN

In the beginning, adjusting to the new reality was incredibly challenging. My emotions were in turmoil, entangled with feelings of apprehension and unease. I longed for someone to confide in to help me navigate the complexities of this deployment. Despite this, the unwavering support of my family and friends, particularly Giselle and Nahla, brought a semblance of solace during this time. Our ladies' nights and spa days, which became cherished rituals, were more than just activities.

They were a lifeline, providing some relief from the ache of missing my husband. The daily exchange of emails with Trevor proved to be an invaluable lifeline throughout this deployment. Due to unreliable phone service, our phone conversations could have been more frequent. Nonetheless, I remain optimistic, knowing that my husband will soon be back home where he belongs.

Six long months had passed, and it was the much-anticipated day. Trevor, my beloved, is finally returning home! The excitement bubbling inside me is akin to a child on Christmas morning. I meticulously prepared myself for his arrival, ensuring every detail was perfect. I adorned myself with striking six-inch pumps, a well-fitted t-shirt, and blue jeans that lovingly embrace my curves. I let my hair down and applied a subtle hint of makeup. Eager for his return, I drove to the airport alone, yearning to have him all myself. The anticipation of being in his arms was almost overwhelming.

A swarm of butterflies fluttered in my stomach as I navigated the exit from Interstate 285 toward the airport. Despite my nervousness, which was a mix of excitement and anxiety, I parked my car and ventured into the airport.

As I made my way through the bustling airport, I couldn't ignore the lingering stares from the men around. Their unabashed attention made me uneasy, so I hastened toward the terminal. Glancing at the arrival board, I noted that I had arrived ahead of schedule; Trevor's flight had just landed. Hurrying to the gate, I allowed myself a few moments to freshen up before his arrival.

As I waited by the gate, a surge of anxiety washed over me. Suddenly, a crowd of people gathered around, obstructing my view. I stood on my toes, trying to catch a glimpse of Trevor amidst the sea of faces, but soon gave up and resignedly waited for him to emerge from the crowd. Finally, I spotted him, dressed in jeans and a T-shirt, carrying a green and brown duffle bag. As he drew nearer, I felt my excitement grow, mirrored in the gleam of his eyes. As we embraced, I felt relief and silently whispered, "Thank you, God."

Despite Trevor just returning from a lengthy and challenging assignment, excitement and uncertainty filled the upcoming month. First, we eagerly anticipated our long-awaited and much-needed honeymoon in the breathtaking destination of Turks & Caicos for a week. Then, embark on our new chapter in Washington, D.C., as Trevor transitioned to his new office which would become our home for the next four years.

I was filled with apprehension and excitement as I left behind my established life and career at a financial firm in Atlanta to support Trevor and his dreams. Along with these changes, we invited my younger brother from Florida to live with us, adding another layer of complexity to our transition. Although we decided to drive separately for cost-cutting, the 10-hour journey could be more convenient.

Trevor's new position means we can afford a more luxurious lifestyle. We bought a vintage two-bedroom condo in Georgetown, an hour from his job. Trevor insisted on buying rather than renting even though we would only be here for four years due to his career. The condo boasts oversized windows, vaulted ceilings, and designer-grade finishes, making me eager to unpack and settle in.

I almost forgot that Trevor and I were expecting our first child - a little girl! We discovered the news shortly after our move, and although it was unexpected, we were thrilled.

The last couple of months have been harsh. I've been feeling sick all day and can't keep anything down. Even the smell of food makes me run to the bathroom. It feels like I'm spending more time with my head in the toilet than anything else. I hoped the all-day sickness didn't last for my entire pregnancy.

At the same time, I was looking forward to meeting the little person growing inside me. The feelings of movement inside me were so unique that I would do anything to continue experiencing them even after my daughter was born. But I couldn't deny that, along with my excitement, there was extreme anxiety about not knowing what would happen in the coming months. I hoped I would be a great mom. The baby books and doctor visits didn't seem to ease my worry, especially since the doctor said I'd have to have a cesarean; I suffered from a complete placenta previa. Despite these challenges, I'm determined to stay positive and focus on the joy of motherhood. I planned to take each day as it came and rely on the support of my loved ones to get through this.

December 8th, a day that will forever be etched in my heart, started like any other. Trevor had already left for work, and I was preparing my favorite meal of eggs. The plan was to spend the day with my brother. But as I stepped out of the shower, a sudden, warm, wet sensation running down my leg jolted me. Panic surged through me as I realized it was blood. I called out for my brother, Keith, who came rushing in, his presence a comforting reassurance. While he called Trevor, I dialed 9-1-1 and stayed on the line with the operator until the paramedics arrived, my mind racing with fear and worry.

The only thing on my mind was the well-being of my daughter. I urgently contacted my auntie and godmother to inform them about the situation. My godmother's voice was reassuring and a blessing as she helped me stay calm. While I was on the phone with her, sirens grew louder, so I stood in the doorway, anxiously waiting. Witnessing the commotion, my neighbor and her husband rushed out to support me just as my dear friend Megan arrived. Once my godmother learned I had others with me, she called Trevor to check on his proximity. Reflecting on the event, I am grateful for having such a strong and dependable support system in place.

"Ma'am, can you tell me what happened?" the young paramedic asks. I explained what had happened and informed them that I had a high-risk pregnancy. Without hesitation, they put me into the ambulance. As they were putting me in, Trevor pulled up. I heard him say, "Keith, come on. We are going to follow behind them."

While in the ambulance, I expressed my concerns to the paramedic, "The last time she moved was last night. I had back pain and called my doctor's office. They just told me to take Tylenol. She normally wakes me up in the morning to eat."

"I am sure she is okay. Try to calm down," the paramedic replied as he was taking my vitals, his empathetic tone did not make me feel better. My mind was racing with worry and fear for my baby while lying in the ambulance heading to the hospital. What was taking us so long to get there? I thought to myself. Each passing minute felt like an eternity as I longed to know if my baby was ok.

As I lay in the hospital bed, a rush of fear and uncertainty flooded over me. The doctors had just informed the nurse to prepare the OR for an emergency C-section due to complications with my pregnancy. I felt a mix of emotions – worry for my baby's well-being, anxiety about the surgery, and a sense of helplessness. I tried to call out to Tre and tell him our baby girl was dead, but the word did not make it out. It was a surreal moment as I was quickly rushed to the OR and prepped for the operating room, surrounded by a blur of medical staff and equipment. The medical staff did not pay my husband or brother any mind or inform them of what they were doing.

While in the operating room, my anxieties were high. I was panicking because I knew that our baby was gone. The nurse was trying to put the oxygen mask on me, but I felt like she was trying to suffocate me. I struggled with her wanting to wait, but she refused. The old lady had the strength of ten men. Before long, my body gave in without my permission. The other nurse put medicine in my IV, which quickly sedated me.

(3 hours later)

"Sweetie, wake up. It's all over. Can you hear me?" the voice of the older nurse started to come through. I was not sure how much time had passed or what happened. I nod to her groggily. Going in and out, I could hear her talking to someone. I wasn't sure who, but that was the least of my concerns.

"Come on in, dear. Trinity still struggles to wake up due to the medicine, but she is okay."

"Trinity. Trinity," the familiar voice called out.

"Trevor, where is she? Is she okay?" I said as I built up the strength to speak and stay conscious for answers.

"No, baby, but you need to rest. I will tell you everything." He kisses me gently and walks out, leaving me in suspense.

I lay there with tears streaming down my cheeks as I slowly drifted back to sleep. Sometime later, I opened my eyes to find my mother-in-law praying over me as the nurse wheeled me into the ICU. Visitors were allowed in once I was settled in the room and had all the necessary monitors attached. But I didn't feel up to visitors or false sympathies. I was still trying to rouse myself from the fog of sleep. The looks of confusion on everyone's faces made it clear that they didn't know how to approach me. I wasn't behaving like a typical grieving mother or someone who had just lost their child. Having experienced the deaths of four loved ones within a year and a half, I had become adept at concealing my emotions. This feeling only served to deepen the misunderstanding and isolation I felt.

One of the ICU nurses asked if I wanted to see my baby, but I declined. I thought that not seeing her would make it hurt less or help me forget the whole experience. I was trying so hard to block out the entire ordeal from my mind. It's challenging to come to terms with the fact that I spent eight months caring for this little person, feeling her kick and move, only to leave empty-handed. It's like winning a race and having someone drop your trophy before you receive it. You were so close. I'm not trying to compare my baby to a race, but I think you understand what I mean.

A day has passed, and I am still in this ICU room. For me to be moved or discharged, I must do something alone. Did I forget to mention that I am also on my third bag of blood? I know it's serious, but I think that the meds and my child's loss give me disillusion as to how severe my health is now. I kept questioning myself, wondering if I could have done anything differently to change the tragic outcome. I would be lying if I said I enjoyed staying in this prison called a hospital. How can one start to heal with the constant pricking and poking from inconsiderate nurses? Plus, the continuous beeping of this heart monitor is rather irritating. How do people sleep with it on?

The nurse entered the room, breaking me out of my thoughts. She was about five feet tall, had red hair, and had a pear-shaped body. She had to be in her mid-fifties. I could tell she had a negative disposition when she entered my room.

"When will I be able to go home?" I asked.

"Mrs. Johnson, if you want to leave and go home. Then you will have to flatulence and bathe yourself," the nurse said aggressively.

She had no remorse regarding my situation. Did this lady not realize that I had just lost my child and nearly died myself, all due to a complicated childbirth?

"Can you bring me a ginger ale and some toiletries, please?" As she left, I found solace in my connection with God, asking Him to help me through this nightmare. Help me push through the pain, the loss of my daughter, and my broken heart.

She left the room and returned within fifteen minutes, placing everything on the table before walking out and closing the curtain. She didn't ask if I needed assistance or stay to ensure I could manage. I slowly sat in bed and let my legs hang off the side. As I reached for the bed rail and stepped down, the pain from the C-section felt like someone was ripping my stomach open. The gas in my stomach made it even worse. If I wanted to go home, I had to do what the nurse said. Tears began to roll down my face, but I forced myself to keep going, thinking about going home. The longer I stood, the harder I cried. "Where is my husband?" I thought. "I need him. I want to go home."

With no one to help me, I struggled with the pain and the difficulty of the moment; all I know is to find solace in my faith and turn to God for strength. Tears streaming down my face, I whispered, "Lord, please help me." I knew that I needed the strength to get through tonight.

As I slowly opened my eyes, a new nurse stood beside me, checking my vitals. She looked at me with a sympathetic expression and gently broke the news that the machine responsible for dispensing my much-needed pain medication was malfunctioning. All this time, every press of the button had been in vain, and the excruciating pain had gone untreated. It felt like an unbearable form of suffering that I had been enduring unknowingly.

Finally, two days later, I made it back to the comfort of home. I'm eagerly anticipating the visit of my aunt and uncle, who are just a few hours away. Unfortunately, due to my recent C-section, I'm unable to engage in any strenuous activities or climb stairs, and it's incredibly frustrating. Usually, I'm an active person, so constantly resting and not being able to do much is getting to me. I'm tired of just sleeping and sitting around; it feels like I'm back in the hospital. I waited until Trevor fell asleep to sneak upstairs to glimpse at the baby pictures. It will be my first time seeing her, and I can't wait. It hurts too much for me to look at her while in the hospital.

"Keith, come here!"

"Yeah," he replied.

"Can you help me upstairs to the computer?"

Once I reached the computer chair, my brother entered his room. I opened up the email with the pictures of the baby. The images hit me like a ton of bricks. At first, I was numb, but as I kept going through the photos, the pain and heartbreak became overwhelming, and I couldn't hold back the tears. "This is my baby, my daughter. I was supposed to protect her. I should have known something was not right the night before."

"I am so sorry, Rosalyn. Mommy should have protected you. But, Lord, why did You let this happen? Why my baby? Am I so horrible that I did not deserve her?"

As tears streamed down my face, I couldn't tear my gaze away from my beautiful baby girl, a perfect blend of her father and me. At that moment, I found myself collapsed on the floor, clutching my stomach and wailing over the loss of my daughter. The sound of my anguished cries brought my husband and brother rushing into the room to see what had happened.

"What happened? Are you okay?" Trevor asked.

"No, why her and not me? My baby," I cried.

"Get up and let me take you back downstairs. How did you get up here?" Trevor said with a tone of frustration.

"I asked Keith to help me. I wanted to see her. I needed to see her."

"You do not need to be putting yourself through this. Rest and relax; you just got home. Your body has been through a lot."

Then Trevor looked over at my brother. "Don't take her back upstairs. Let me know what she wants, and I will get it for her." Trevor tried to console me, but the loss of our daughter was too much to bear. So, I lay in his arms and cried myself to sleep.

There were times when I imagined what it would be like to hold my baby for the first time. As I lay in the hospital bed, exhausted from labor, the nurse finally placed my tiny daughter in my arms. As the days turned into weeks and months, I could not help but think about each milestone my baby would have achieved; her first smile, babbling sounds, and attempts at crawling made my heart swelled with pride.

Chapter Six

THE STORM

Chapter Six
THE STORM

Two years of coping with the loss of our daughter was an arduous journey. While endeavoring to move forward, I found it emotionally distressing to encounter expectant mothers or learn of others' experiences with childbirth. At times, I found myself questioning the reasons behind our loss and experiencing emotional fragility, matters that Trevor did not fully comprehend. Consequently, his ability to manage my fluctuating emotional states was affected. We both were putting our emotions to work, and we were surprised when we found out we were pregnant again.

I remember it like it was yesterday when Dr. Lane wanted to take my entire uterus out. She told me it was shredded, and they did their best to put it back together. But the unwavering support of healthcare professionals like Dr. Hunter made all the difference. He kept reassuring me throughout my pregnancy that everything would be ok, even informing his colleagues about my condition, just in case he was out. I was so grateful for his dedication because when he was on leave, Reign decided to make her debut. My symptoms started out like my previous pregnancy, with back aches. When I called the on-call doctor, they wanted me to come in just to make sure everything was ok. Luckily, I was at the hospital when my water broke because I had the same issue with Reign that I did with Rosalyn. Everything went smoothly during my delivery, except that Reign decided to shower the doctor with her urine.

Trevor and I had agreed that I would take on the role of a stay-at-home mother until our daughter Reign was old enough for school. As a result, my days were spent at home, caring for our adorable daughter and managing the household. While the initial months were fulfilling, I yearned for corporate America's stimulating conversations and fast-paced environment.

Trevor and I had devoted little time to each other. That realization caused me to suggest we plan a much-needed date night. However, just as I brought up the idea, my phone rang. "Hey Trevor, I was just thinking of you. We should have a date night tonight," I suggested with anticipation.

To my disappointment, Trevor responded, "Not tonight. I was calling to let you know that I have to work late, and I will be too exhausted tomorrow."

I felt let down and lonely; I replied, "Oh, okay. See you when you get home. I love you."

"Yeah, me too, bye," and he just hung the phone up.

My woman's intuition began to start; something was not adding up. Trevor always said, "I love you" back. And around that time, when I mentioned sex, he just blew it off. I gained some weight since the baby was born, but I was not that bad. Or was I? When I needed direction, I always called on the one person I knew had my back. "Lord, please give me the strength to deal with whatever is going on. If my husband is up to something, please bring it to light."

Throughout the night, I lay in bed, the covers twisting around me as I anxiously awaited Trevor's return. I must have drifted off at some point because I was abruptly roused by the sound of keys fumbling at the front door. I glanced over at the old alarm clock on the dresser; its glowing numbers displayed 2 am. It struck me odd that he would return from work at this hour, which sent me a jolt of surprise. I feigned sleep as he quietly undressed and settled into bed, waiting until his resounding, rhythmic snores filled the room before I dared to move. I grab his phone and go into the living room. Once I unlocked his phone, I saw what I assumed all alone. There were text messages and pictures between Trevor and another woman.

I jumped up, stormed into the bedroom, and hurled the phone at my husband's head. Trevor jolted up in shock as the realization of being caught dawned on him. I stood there, trembling with a mixture of anger, hurt, and disappointment, with my eyes locked onto his with an intensity that made him falter. Words failed me as the weight of betrayal settled in my chest, leaving me breathless and shattered. I didn't know how to pick up the pieces because my world was turned upside down.

"Trinity? What happened? What's wrong?"

"So, you've been having an affair with your intern?" I managed to utter, my voice trembling with disbelief and shock.

In response, Trevor dismissively said, "Man, what are you talking about? I was asleep, and you woke me up for suspicion," as he rolled over to sleep.

"Trevor, who is she?" I demanded, my voice unwavering and relentless, a mix of anger and hurt seeping through.

"Before you lie, I read all the text messages and emails, including the last one, which confirms she was the one you were with. So, are you having an affair? Are you willing to risk it all for some naive 20-year-old?"

Ignoring my questions, Trevor got out of bed and walked into the living room as if I had not asked him anything. Fueled by frustration and a deep sense of betrayal, I followed him, my heart heavy with the weight of his actions.

"Hello, I'm talking to you," I said as I put my hands on my hips.

"I don't care. Leave me alone, Trinity. I just want to be by myself."

"There is no leaving you alone. You have to be out of your mind. How about I call your boss and let him know how you mingle with the intern? Or, better yet, send an email to everyone at your job. You don't care about me or the marriage."

"Are you making threats, Trinity? Try me if you want; you will not have to worry about me. Now leave me alone."

I grabbed his phone and called his mistress. Yeah, to me, she is everything except a child of God. "Hello. This is Trinity, Trevor's wife. It would help me understand what is happening between you all."

The Other Woman

It was a bizarre turn of events as my husband made me feel like the "*other woman*." The intern initially tried to play innocent, insisting that their relationship was strictly professional. However, I quickly shattered her facade by mentioning the incriminating text messages and explicit photos I had discovered.

As the conversation escalated, my husband intervened and shockingly defended his mistress, urging me not to sabotage her internship. His unexpected defense of her and proclamation of love left me feeling betrayed and cast aside. At that moment, I couldn't help but feel like an outsider in my marriage, as if I were the one jeopardizing someone else's happiness. It was a profoundly disorienting and painful experience to realize that the person I loved was choosing someone else over me.

My heart shattered as I heard my husband's words echoing in my mind. Did he just confess his love for his mistress? I stood frozen, unable to process the heartbreaking revelation. As I dropped his phone in shock, he casually picked it up and dialed, speaking as if I were invisible to his friend, and walked outside.

From the other end of the line, I could hear his friend urgently advising him to salvage his marriage before risking his career by calling his boss. The words pierced through me, and I was in tears, sitting on the edge of our bed. The pain was unbearable. How could he betray me like this? I had given him everything, only to be treated with such disregard.

When he finally entered the room and sat at the end of the bed, I could see the weight of his words in his eyes. "I'm sorry, I never meant to hurt you," he said quietly. All I could feel was a deep sense of betrayal and disbelief. It felt like my whole world was crumbling around me.

I couldn't help but feel shocked and hurt by the way Trevor was acting. How could he tell me he needed space as if we were just dating? Doesn't he realize that I'm *his wife* and this is not a game? I tried to reason with him and save our marriage for days, but Trevor's mind was already made up. I was so exhausted from all of this that the only thing I could think to do was to text my godfather about the situation and then just go to sleep.

Chapter Seven

WELCOME BACK TO ATLANTA

WELCOME BACK TO ATLANTA

Six months had passed since the devastating night when I discovered my husband's infidelity with his young mistress. Despite my longing to reconcile and save our marriage, Trevor seemed to have moved on. Nevertheless, I returned to Atlanta, where Mr. Jameson graciously allowed me to regain my previous job. Now, my daughter, Reign, and I have settled into a spacious three-bedroom townhouse in Duluth, Georgia, approximately 40 minutes from downtown Atlanta. My brother started his freshman year at Georgia State University. I am so glad for him to be close by.

Talk to God

The journey has been incredibly challenging, but I have found solace in my unwavering faith. My brother has been my pillar of support, especially when caring for Reign, and he remains the only one with whom I have shared my innermost thoughts and feelings. One day, in a moment of despair after learning that Trevor had relocated his mistress into our former home, my daughter witnessed my anguish and tried her best to comfort me. "Mommy, what's wrong?" Reign asked as she enveloped me in a warm embrace. Then she lovingly added, "If you can't talk to me, you can talk to God."

Her simple words marked a pivotal moment that allowed me to unburden myself of the pain and heartache I had been carrying. I threw myself into work and spent precious time with my brother and daughter. On some evenings, I sought refuge in conversations with a mutual friend of Trevor and mine, who was also grappling with his challenges. Despite his friendship with my husband, he became a source of humor and encouragement, evolving into a confidant who provided much-needed support.

"Hey, mate, what's the plan?" Tony inquired. Tony always found a way to cheer me up and encourage me to move on.

"Nothing, about to head out with Nahla for a girl's night. She wants to go out, but I am not in the mood."

"You need to go and enjoy yourself. "

"Well, if I go out, you gotta tell the neighbor your name."

We both laughed because it was an inside joke about his neighbor playing a particular song so loud as if she was trying to hint.

"Okay, I got you." I knew he was lying but said OKAY, and we hung up.

Before heading downtown, I met Nahla at a seafood restaurant she wanted to try. As we walked into the restaurant, this tall, slightly framed man who looked boyish approached us.

"How can I help you, ladies?" he asked, holding a pen and notepad.

"I know what you're thinking, but that's not on the menu," Nahla teased, earning a playful jab in the ribs from me.

"Did you say something?" the waiter replied. With a playful twinkle in my eye, I said, "Don't mind her. Can we both get the special, please?" Our exchange was laced with a hint of flirtation, adding an intriguing element to our interaction.

"Okay, I will put your order in," the waiter interjected, momentarily breaking the flow of our conversation and surprising us with his sudden but not unwelcome interruption.

We walked over to a table and sat down. The plan was to dine in and then head to a jazz lounge. While waiting for our food, we caught up on some small talk, discussing our week and the latest gossip. I couldn't help but notice how the waiter and my eyes kept meeting. I quickly put my head down when I noticed he was looking. I didn't want to make it evident that I was scoping him out. Nahla should have seen what was happening because she was too busy telling me about some new guy she met.

Small talk quickly stopped when the waiter brought over our drinks. As her loving, outspoken self, Nahla said, "Thank you, um. I don't want to say, sir, what is your name?"

He laughed with amusement, "My name is Robert. "Well, thank you, Robert.

"Does Robert have a girlfriend, wife, or boyfriend?" Nahla asked.

"Nahla!" I said in disbelief. I couldn't believe she said that, but we were in Atlanta. You have to be careful here.

"No, I don't have any of those. I work a lot to get my restaurant up and running," Robert said.

"Your restaurant? He owns this restaurant, and he doesn't have a girlfriend, wife, or boyfriend, so girl, you better jump on that," Nahla said unapologetically.

My face turned red. I couldn't believe what Nahla had just done. This man probably thinks I'm desperate or a freak. I'm still legally married because Trevor refused to sign the divorce papers. Then, to my surprise, Robert asked if we could exchange numbers. Without second-guessing it, we did. Robert and I were texting back and forth as we ate our food. We decided to meet up next weekend, something very casual. Nahla and I were so busy talking and stuffing our faces that we missed the show, so we decided to call it a night.

As I got ready for work, my aunt called to find out what happened between Trevor and me. Since I left my husband, I have been more secretive with my moves and genuinely dealing with my marriage.

"Trinity, how are you, Keith, and Reign doing?"

"We are good. They are in the living room, and I am about to go to work."

"I do not know what is wrong with Trevor. He is so…" Before she could finish, I had to stop her, "Auntie, do not say anything negative about him. Despite what he did, he still is the father of my child. God said to leave it alone, not call or get upset, so I will let God deal with him. I am about to go. I will talk to you later. Love you, bye."

"Love you too."

This was the same scenario with family and friends when they discovered what happened in my marriage. They want to know if I'm filing for divorce or putting him on child support. Their questions were why I was so low-key and focused on what's essential, my daughter.

As I walked out the door, my phone rang. I reach into my purse and out of all people, Trevor was facetiming me! "Reign, your daddy is on the phone," I called to her. My innocent baby girl came running with the biggest smile, her eyes sparkling with excitement at the prospect of seeing her father.

"Hi Daddy, when will I get to see you?"

"Hey there, daddy's girl. It won't be long now. How have you been?" he replied, his voice filled with anticipation.

"I'm good! I just started ballet class this week. Uncle Keith is taking me to the park today. Yay!" she exclaimed with joy in her voice.

I used to attempt to engage my husband in conversations about our marriage, hoping for him to express his desire for me, admit his mistakes, or say he misses me. Unfortunately, these discussions always led to arguments. However, as I observed our child, Reign's excitement during our co-parenting activities, I realized the importance of setting aside my feelings and focusing on co-parenting. This realization has been a significant shift in my priorities.

Additionally, Trevor asked me to continue paying his bills with his money, of course. He needed to figure out what it took to manage the house. Although some may have questioned this arrangement, Trevor wanted me to have access to his bank account for any necessary expenses for us and bill payments. If my daughter were aware of this, they would probably disapprove.

I entrusted my marriage to God and realized I could not change someone or make them want what I wanted. I was focused on my spiritual relationship and striving to be the best mom for our daughter, even if it meant putting my feelings aside occasionally.

"Where is Mommy?" Trevor asked our daughter.

"She is in the kitchen. Mommy! Daddy wants you." Reign hands me the phone and returns to the living room to watch her cartoons.

"Yes, Trevor."

"How have you been?"

"I've had better days, but I'm good," I responded, accepting the situation and showing Trevor that I understood and respected his need to focus on work.

"I have this thing at work with two of my employees, and I want your opinion."

He had come to me with a work issue to talk about before. But that time, I was confused because he mentioned that his mistress had his back. I kissed Reign on the cheek and headed out the door while listening to him. The phone conversation lasted another ten minutes before he abruptly said, "I will call you right back."

As I pulled up to work, I had to pray with tears coming down my eyes, "Dear God, please give me the strength to face the challenges in my life. Help me find the peace and resilience to endure difficult times. Guide me towards making the right decisions and grant me the wisdom to see things through. Amen."

After praying, I felt lighter. I fixed my makeup, composed myself, and then walked into work, focusing on ensuring that the two clients I met with today would sign the contract.

Night out

I called Giselle on my way home from work because I missed her call this morning. She has been calling me every day to check on us. "Hey girl, I just walked into the house. We talked for about 15 minutes before I got off the phone.

After the phone conversation with Giselle about me enjoying life a little, I decided to go on a date with Robert. But first I have to take care my of mommy duty and relaxed with my baby girl for a little while.

I kept it simple with blue jeans, Gucci pumps, and a white T-shirt, and I wore my hair back in a ponytail because I didn't want to give him the wrong impression. Before I left, I kissed Reign goodnight and reassured her that Mommy would be back. Then, I grabbed my purse and headed to Bahamas Breeze to meet Robert.

My mind is racing with many thoughts as I drive to the restaurant. I had not dated in over five years, so I was unsure of how to act. The place seemed crowded, as I walked to the door, the butterflies began to flutter in my stomach. As I opened the door, he stood at the host stand. He looked really good. His outfit was well put together and complemented his figure. He exuded confidence and carried himself with a cheerful demeanor. Overall, he had a very appealing and attractive presence. As our eyes met when I walked in, he was still as sexy as ever with his boyish grin. I think that he read my mind because he was dressed very casually.

"Wow, Trinity, you look stunning. I'm thrilled that you decided to join me," he greeted me warmly, enfolding me in a hug. His scent was incredibly alluring.

"Thank you, Robert. You're not looking too shabby yourself."

We made our way to the table and conversed as though we were old friends catching up. The more we spoke, the more at ease I felt with him. I'm generally reticent about discussing my past marriage, but he created an environment that made it feel natural. He didn't pass judgment; he simply listened. I did not want to dominate the conversation, so I encouraged Mr. Robert to share his thoughts. He didn't boast like many of the men I've dated in the past. Robert disclosed that he used to play professional basketball and was contemplating a return to the sport. Throughout the evening, our dialogue remained lighthearted and enjoyable. It felt like I was again a high school girl, infatuated with the most popular guy in school.

"Excuse me, would you two lovebirds like anything else before I close out your ticket?" the waitress said.

"No, ma'am, thank you. We are good," Robert replied.

As the waitress walked away, we looked at each other and smiled. After Robert paid the bill, we walked to my car. I hugged him and opened the door to get into my vehicle.

"So, you're just going to give me that old church lady hug and jump in your car? Can I get a real one?" he said with a flirtatious smile.

"That was not an old lady hug. You are a mess, but okay." So, as I got out of my car, he pulled me closer to him and kissed me. His hand slowly slid down my back and rested on my butt as we were kissing. The kisses became more intense, and I could tell that his body wanted more than just a kiss.

"Okay, Edmund, I think I need to go," I said as I tried to get it together.

"I don't want you to leave. We can go to my friend's house; he is out of town. We can talk."

There goes that typical guy comment. I thought it was time to leave. But something about the way Robert said it, the sincerity in his voice, made me reconsider. It was as if he genuinely wanted to spend more time with me, to understand me better.

"No, Robert. I will call you tomorrow. Goodnight," I kissed him and got into my car.

"I will be waiting for that phone call," he said as he shut my door.

My thoughts were filled with Robert as I drove home. His embrace was so comforting, and the feeling of being wanted by a man was powerful. It validated my worth, that I hadn't experienced in four years. It made me question when the last time Trevor made me feel so alive.

As I pulled into my driveway, my train of thought was interrupted by my phone ringing. I couldn't help but wonder if it was Robert.

"Hello, sir."

"Oh, sir?" Robert laughed. "I just wanted to make sure you made it home, beautiful."

"Yes, I just pull up. Thank you for checking on me."

"You're welcome. Have a good night, and I will talk to you later."

"Goodnight," and we hung up.

The Next Day

Giselle walked in while I was sitting at my desk, humming a happy tune.

"Well, somebody had an amazing night."

"Yes, it was." I stop typing as I look up at her. She had a big grin on her face.

"So, give me all the juicy details, and I mean ALL," she said as she sat in the chair before my desk.

So, I started talking about my night with Robert. We were talking and our laughter filling the air when the receptionist interrupted by beeping in with an urgent call from the office.

"Um, Trinity, you have a call on line one," Jennifer said in a snarky tone. I couldn't help but stifle a laugh as I watched Giselle's spot-on imitation of her.

"Thank you, send it through," I said, my curiosity piqued.

(Pause)

"Hello, this is Trinity. How may I help you?"
"Meet me at my place tonight," a male voice responded.
"Excuse me?"

"You forgot about me already. I guess last night I did not do a great job."

" Robert?"

Giselle couldn't help but make a kissing face as she watched me talk to Robert on the phone.

"Yes, so can I see you tonight?"

"You want to see me tonight at your place? Um…" Giselle made her way around my desk to listen. Then she motioned for me to agree. With my hand on the receiver, I kept shaking my head. My mind kept telling me it was not a good idea, but my mouth said, "Yes."

"Great, I will see you tonight. I will text you later," he said.

"Okay, see you then," he replied before hanging up. After ending the call, I rested my head in my hands for a few seconds.

"Giselle, what did you get me into? I prefer meeting in a public setting, not an intimate one. You know what that could lead to," I expressed my concern.

"Oh yes, just what the doctor ordered," she said as she danced seductively. "You can thank me later by giving me all the details. Bye!" she said as she walked out of my office. I just shook my head and dove back into my laptop.

It was 1 pm, so I decided to call Trevor and see if we could discuss moving forward with a divorce or reconciling our marriage.

"Hello," a female voice answered Trevor's house phone.

"Uh, Hello? I dialed the wrong number," I said. As I was about to hang up, the female replied, "No, you didn't. Trevor is not here."

As she kept talking, I recognized the familiar voice. It was Trevor's mistress. But I could not understand why she was in the house when he was not there.

"Where is Trevor, and why are you there?" I asked.

"He is at work, and I live here," she said. I could feel her pride coming through the phone. She wanted me to know that she was living there. Did this man just throw his wife and daughter out like garbage and move his mistress in?! I was boiling on the inside, but I refused to let her know.

So, I just played it cool, and I explained to her that she would never be able to walk two steps in my shoes because I was the one who made him who he was. Clearly, a child like herself could never understand what it takes to be Trevor's wife or understand marriage because if she did, she would not tell a man to leave his family to be with her and expect a fairytale ending.

"Tell Trevor to call me".

Trevor possessed an uncanny ability to convince a rational person to purchase four flat tires, especially if they were unfamiliar with him. I felt like I knew him better than his mother. After I hung up the phone, I was consumed by an overwhelming sense of anger. I attempted to give myself time to calm down, repeating the mantra, "God, grant me the strength because I don't think I can go on like this." The need for support was tangible. After uttering it the third time, my phone ringing rudely interrupted my moment.

"Hello?"

"Why are you repeatedly calling my house and threatening her? Stop trying to threaten her and bully me. Respect our privacy, allowing us to live in peace."

"RESPECT? Nigga, sign the divorce papers, pay the child support and alimony. I am not holding you back; I signed my part and sent you the papers. You have some nerve. You need some time alone. But you have that woman living in the house I picked out."

"She doesn't live there. She stops by to see my roommate while I'm at work."

"You're lying again. Since you won't sign the papers, I will file for child support and alimony to support my child. Then, when I have enough for an attorney, I will get my divorce."

"If you put me on child support, don't say anything else to me unless it's about our daughter," and he abruptly hung up.

The phone call with Trevor and his mistress felt like a sudden storm, wreaking havoc on my day and leaving everything in disarray. As I drove home, I couldn't shake off the replay of the painful scenario in my head. It's crystal clear that Trevor didn't want a break to work on our marriage; he just wanted to be with his mistress. If he's so into her, why the hell was he dragging his feet on signing the divorce papers? I was even considering finding a way to make extra money for an attorney. I just wanted him out of my life, and I was starting to feel like I didn't even want him in our daughter's life. It's all just so frustrating. I am so glad that Keith took Reign to the zoo for her play date. I did not want her to see me upset. I called to check on them and let Keith know where I was going. I took a shower, got dressed, and jumped into the car.

As I pulled up to Robert's apartment, my phone rang. I was not in the mood to talk, but I instantly answered as I looked at the caller ID.

"Hey, Tony."

"Hey, friend, why do you sound down?"

"It's a long story and it has to do with your friend and his mistress/intern."

"What happened now?" I went on to explain what happened this morning. From how quiet he was on the phone; I could tell that Tony was more in disbelief than I was.

"Man, what is Trevor thinking? I wanted you all to get back together so bad."

"Ding ding, that's the number one question. That girl is young enough to be dating my baby brother. Like I told him, he probably is having a midlife crisis, or he is a weak-ass man. When you are sneaking around, it is all fun and special until you have to deal with that person daily. The little girl has no clue about a relationship or commitment, let alone a marriage. She wants to live my life because she thinks I have it all. Being married to your friend is not all glitz and glamor. I work for this lifestyle."

"I'm sorry that you are going through this. You are a good wife and mother. I don't know what's wrong with him."

"Do you know this fool had the nerve to tell her that he had never been in love until now!"

"Wow."

"Right, I'm supposed to meet up with Robert tonight, but I am not in the mood."

"Man, get out and enjoy yourself. You don't need to sit at home worrying about them."

"I know, but I'm torn. I don't feel right going on a date while still married. Nor do I want to lead someone on," I confessed, my voice betraying my inner turmoil.

"It's just a date, not a marriage proposal. Go have some fun with the basketball player, Stella," Tony laughed.

"Go ask the neighbor if she knows your name so she can stop playing the song."

Then we both laughed. Talking to Tony is like a breath of fresh air. He always knows what to say to cheer me up. Regarding a relationship, we have the same idea of what it should be. Before we hung up, we talked about what he was going through and how he was ready to return to the East Coast.

Sitting outside of Robert's place, I tried to calm my nerves. I took one last deep breath and checked my makeup. "Yep, Trinity, everything is in place." I made my way toward his door, my heart racing with anticipation. As I knocked, my stomach fluttered with butterflies. And just then, the door swings open, with Robert standing there in basketball shorts and a smile.

I thought to myself, "He is sexy with his shirt off. I guess Tony is right. I'll just call myself Stella tonight." But as I stepped inside, I couldn't help but feel a pang of guilt. Was I ready for this? For a new relationship?

"Hey, gorgeous, come on in," Robert said as he hugged me.

Being in his arms feels so good. Please don't let go, I think to myself. Robert 's voice brought me back into reality. "Hey, I just moved here, so please excuse the lack of furniture," he said as he pulled away.

"Oh, no problem," I replied, sitting on the black barrel swivel chair. It had enough room for two people to get cozy.

"I hope you don't mind, but I will shower quickly."

"No problem."

As Robert walked toward his bathroom, he playfully said, "Don't try to come in and get a sneak peek."

"Boy, stop," I said, and we both laughed.

After about five minutes, I was tempted to get a sneak peek. "Hmm, WWGD, what would Giselle do?" I thought to myself. Without hesitation, I quickly dashed toward the bathroom. Peeking from around the corner of the door, I had a fantastic view. Tilting my head sideways, I thought to myself, "Wow! This man is fine. I need to thank his mother for birthing something like that. Not one ounce of fat."

"So", Robert glanced back again, taking me by surprise. "Are you going to keep peeking around the corner, or will you join me?" he said with a mischievous smile.

"Uh, I came to ask if I could get a glass of water," I replied, a bit embarrassed.

"Sure, help yourself," he chuckled. "Thank you," I said as I quickly approached the kitchen.

Ten more minutes passed until Edmund strolled into the living room. I tried to hide my embarrassment from our previous interaction as I sipped on my water and focused on the infomercial playing on the TV.

"So, did you like what you saw?" he asked with a smirk as he sat beside me. "It was alright, not bad for a youngin," I said with a shrug, trying to downplay my earlier embarrassment.

"Oh, youngin?! So, we are going to throw out the age card?" he replied as he laughed. "But this cougar next to me was staring hard."

"Whatever, so what movie are we going to watch?"

"How about Love and Basketball?" I just look at him and laugh.

Robert got comfortable and put his arm around me. About 35 minutes into the movie, he began kissing my neck. I tried to resist, but after 10 minutes, I gave in. His kisses were so sweet and passionate. Before long, we gave the movie some competition. Edmond slid his hand under my skirt, but before he could go further, I stopped him and pushed him away.

"Did I do something wrong?" he questioned as his nose and forehead scrunched up, one eyebrow raised higher than the other, and pursed lips.

"No, the timing is wrong. I don't want to lead you on. I'm sorry, I got to go," I replied, staring at the floor. I gather my things and head out the door.

Surprisingly, he walked behind me, ensuring I got to my car safely. The action made me look at him in another light; he is such a gentleman. I thought, why couldn't I have met him before I met Trevor?

"Call me when you make it home, Trinity." Without looking back at him, I said, "Ok." and jumped into my car.

I observed as Robert walked back into his house. I couldn't believe he had stepped outside wearing only his boxers. Five minutes went by, and I still needed to start my car. I kept replaying Tony's words: "You only live once, T. And besides, do you think Trevor is at home worrying about you?" So, I took a deep breath, exited my car, and returned to Robert's door. I knocked on the door with hesitation. There was a long pause, which made me start thinking negative thoughts.

As Robert opened the door, a perplexed expression washed over his face. Without exchanging a word, I slipped by him and entered the house. The unsettled look on his face suggested that his thoughts were in turmoil. Placing my purse on the chair, I advanced further into the room. Unexpectedly, I initiated a passionate kiss without uttering a single word. It was a bold move; unlike anything I had done before.

Yes, I was aggressive for the first time. Maybe I had a lot of bottled-up emotions; who knows? Edmund did not fight back. It felt like he could feel what I was thinking. The vibe was sensual and hot. The chemistry between us was undying and electrifying. Without breaking from kissing, I wrapped my arms around his neck as he gripped the back of my thighs and lifted me. He carried me to the bed and gently laid on it.

"Are you sure that you want to do this?"

I reached to pull him toward me, looking at him in his eyes and answering with kisses. At that moment, he slid off my clothes and stared at me, and I was puzzled as to why he stopped.

"Your body is amazing, Trinity," he said as he resumed kissing me. "Tonight is only about you and me; nothing else matters." Then he began to kiss me all over. His kisses just made me want him even more. His kisses seem to melt away my frustration and pain. At that moment, he made me feel like my need and attention was the only thing that mattered. After what felt like an eternity, I did not want him to stop. No guy has ever made my body crave for it over and over, not even Trevor. But trust me, he was not on my mind at that. Robert and I lay there for a while before I decided to leave.

"Okay, give me a kiss before I walk you out," he requested, and that kiss led to an unexpected hour of shared intimacy.

Regardless of how late it is, I refuse to let my daughter wake up in the morning without me being home!

Since last night, Robert has called me three times, even this morning before I reached my workplace, to wish me a good day. I cherish the attention he showers on me. Despite his young age, he exudes a remarkable maturity.

"Well, who's got you smiling so much this Monday?"

Before I could turn around in my chair, I recognized the voice of the heavily accented Jamaican woman, Giselle, a mysterious figure who always seemed to know more than she let on.

"Hey, Giselle, how are you?"

"I'm good, but not as good as you. So, will you give me all the juicy details since you forgot to call me last night when you were home?"

"Who said I went home? Besides, a woman does not kiss and tell. Bye, Giselle," I said as I put my head down to pretend, I was looking at the files on my desk.

"Ok, I'll wait for you to tell me", she smirks as she walks out of my office.

My relationship with Robert was developing beautifully. Over time, we found many common interests, such as a love for horseback riding and trying new foods. We were not in a romantic relationship but more like friends with benefits. He hadn't met Reign, and I preferred to keep it that way. When I was with Robert, I could become different and leave all the hurt and pain behind. He understood my daughter will always be my first priority and I have been very transparent with him about my marriage situation.

Robert called me to say he would be leaving in two weeks to play overseas basketball. He said he would keep in touch, but I knew that was a lie. I wished him well. I was a little disappointed, but I knew he was just something for the moment. We had a ten-year age difference and were in two different places in our lives. I would be a fool to think there could've been more. At least I will get to see him off before he leaves.

I wanted to blow off some stress and Reign's energy. I wish I could bottle her energy up and sell it. So, I took her to the gym. She was ecstatic to visit the children's area, her favorite spot in the whole gym.

"Hey, sweetie, how about we have a special mommy-daughter day?" I suggested.

"Okay, mommy. Can we go to the park or the zoo?" Reign asked, her bright brown eyes filled with excitement.

"How about we go to the gym first and then the park?" I proposed.

"YES!" Reign exclaimed, her enthusiasm contagious. Then, she lowered her head and added, "Mommy, I wish Daddy could come with us."

"I know, baby, but Daddy has to work. We can call him tonight," I assured her. It's always challenging to explain the situation to her, considering she's so young. I don't want to portray her father negatively, so I choose my words carefully.

"Okay, mommy," Reign replied with a smile that warmed my heart.

Once I arrived at the gym, I was able to drop off Reign at the kids' club and hop on the elliptical without the married trainer noticing me. I needed to figure out who was spreading the rumor that I needed a man. I love coming to the gym; it helps me clear my mind. I get a whole hour to focus on myself – no job hunting, no mommy duties, just me.

About 30 minutes into my workout, I was surprised to see my ex. Atlanta was too small. He was still as attractive as ever. We dated while we were in high school. I was a freshman, and he was a senior. Like most high school relationship, they do not last long. Despite how it ended, we always remain cool.

"Hey, Ms. Jones, how are you?"

"I'm doing well. How have you been? I hope everything's going great for you."

"Trying to get a sexy body like you."

"Boy, you are a mess," I replied, shaking my head and laughing. "Where is your girl? I don't want to get you in trouble."

"Whatever, she is over there lifting weights, but I am asking about you. I will stop by tomorrow and visit you and your mini-me."

His girlfriend strolled up as I was on the verge of responding to him. It was puzzling to me what he sees in her because she's the opposite of me. The stark contrast made me wonder about both of their inclinations. Nevertheless, I had no romantic interest in him, so their private pleasures were of no concern to me. I was simply grateful for Chad's friendship and how he made Reign feel cherished. He even went as far as to surprise her with an enchanting pony ride, treating her like royalty.

"Hey, how are you?", I said to Chad's girlfriend.

"Are you ready to go?" his girlfriend asked him without even a hello. I guessed I was invisible or a nonfactor, but the girl must not know. I've already had her man, besides, there is nothing but a friendship between us.

"Ok," he said, looking at her with disbelief. Then he turned to me. "Have a good workout, T." I returned to my zone and continued working out.

I want to clarify something. You might think that I'm living a glamorous life or out here *sluttying* it up surrounded by guys, but that's not true. I've always had more male friends than female friends since high school. I'm not sure if it's because of jealousy or lack of confidence on their part. It may sound like I'm being conceited, but I'm just being honest. I've always had a small waist and a curvy bottom, which is something that many women pay for through cosmetic surgery (BBL). The only difference is that mine is natural. Sometimes I wish I didn't have it because it attracts the wrong kind of attention, and I can never wear a tennis skirt.

After dedicating two hours to a rigorous workout, Reign and I indulged in a well-deserved treat at Genesis's ice cream parlor in Stone Mountain, followed by a delightful afternoon at the park. Our time together was filled with joy, laughter, and precious shared experiences. I passed on the ice cream and opted for a refreshing smoothie. Reign was excited as we explored the park and its scenic trails, chatting animatedly during our stroll.

I'm grateful that the challenges brought about by her father's actions had not dampened Reign's spirits. He was truly missing out on witnessing her remarkable growth.

Observing her animatedly darting from the slide to the swing, I was struck by how her zest for life continues to gleam so brightly. At just four years old, her love and unwavering faith in God captivated me, prompting me to reflect on the biblical verse, Matthew 18.3. The verse speaks of God's appreciation for childlike humility, gentle spirits, joyous hearts, and unwavering faith. Amidst the trials and tribulations of adulthood, I found myself becoming increasingly cynical.

As I've grown older, I have found myself placing more "hurdles of doubt and worry" in my path. It has been a challenge to ignore obstacles that could impede my progress, throw me off balance, or discourage me from nurturing a deeper connection with God. Reign and her steadfast faith have been my guiding light. Her faith has inspired me to conquer my doubts and fears.

After about an hour at the park, we headed home so that I could prepare dinner. As I looked into the rear-view mirror to back, I saw Reign fast asleep. She played hard today. The drive home was quiet, which I usually would not mind. But these past few months, I've been struggling with my thoughts. I was filled with a mix of emotions, regret and sadness. I cannot believe that this man would do this to me. I wish that I never met him, but I am grateful for my daughter. How could he claim to love me but mistreat me? It had been ten months, and I was still filled with many emotions. The more I thought about it, the angrier I got.

Three months ago, I went to DC for a friend's wedding, so I asked Trevor if it was ok for Reign and me to stay with him. He was ok with it until we were enroute. Then, he told me he had a change of heart about me staying there. I could not believe this man said he didn't think I should stay at the house, but I could drop Reign off to spend time. How could he treat the mother of his child like that? The same woman he vowed in front of God to love and respect. Luckily, I was able to get Reign and me a hotel room.

I was unsure if I was dumb or stupid enough to love this man, even after all he had done and how badly he had treated me. I shook my head in disbelief, hoping it would change my thoughts, but unfortunately, it didn't, so I did the only thing I knew best, pray and ask God to work with him and me.

As I was getting my gym bag out, my brother, who was home for the summer from college, walked out.

"Hey, bro-ham, where are you about to go?"

"I am heading to work. Trevor called earlier; he wanted to know where you were. I told him that I didn't know."

"Oh, ok," I will call him later. Can you get Reign out of the car for me while I grab things? Just lay her in her room, please."

"Sure, are you cooking tonight?"

"I thought you were treating us since you are balling," I said as we laughed. "Yes, I am."

He returned from taking Reign inside before I could finish getting everything out of the car. "Bye. Have a good day, Keith."

"Okay, you too."

I headed upstairs to get a quick shower since Reign was taking a nap. After showering, I checked on Reign, but she still sleeping. As I reached into my purse for my phone, I noticed six missed calls and two voicemails from Trevor. I was not in the mood for his pessimism. So, I decided to call him later and went ahead and got dinner started. Before I could head into the kitchen, the doorbell rang. I hurried to answer the door because I did not want the doorbell sound to wake Reign.

"Who is it?"

"It's Robert."

As I opened the door, I was startled. "What are you doing here? You said that you were going to stop by tomorrow?"

"I didn't say that."

"You did, Rob. And why did you not call before you came over? My man could have been here," I said as I started cooking in the kitchen.

"Old girl had a work meeting, so I wanted to come by and see you and Reign."

"*Old girl?* Is that what they call girlfriends nowadays? Ok. I was just about to prepare dinner while Reign was napping."

"How have you been? It's been a while since I last saw you."

"I'm doing okay; I'm just trying to do the best I can in my new role as a single parent."

Rob and I talked about old times and a little about the present. He has always been a person of few words regarding his personal life, and I am used to it, so catching up with him was just a fresh breath of air.

As we were talking, I heard the sound of little footsteps.

"Mommy, mommy, where are you?" she screamed as she walked to the bottom of the stairs.

"I am in the kitchen, Reign."

"Hey Reign, how have you been?"

"Hi, Rob. I have been great! Mommy and I also ate ice cream at the park."

"Did Mommy get on the swing with you too?"

"No," Reign said as she laughed at the thought. "She is too big. Mommy might break the swing."

"What?! Really, Reign," I replied as I looked at her in disbelief. I grabbed her and gave her a big hug and kiss. "Alright, missy, go to the living room and watch TV until I finish dinner."

"Ok, Mommy," she said as she turned toward Rob. "Rob, can you come and play with me?" Rob could never tell her no, so I just watched, smirked, and waited for his response.

"Sure, give me one second with mommy, and I will be right in there," Rob replied.

"Ok!" she said as she skipped into the living room with glee.

"Well, my date is waiting; don't get jealous," he said as he left the kitchen.

Robert stayed and played with Reign for about 30 minutes before going home. I fed Reign, bathed her, and put her to bed. Unfortunately, by the time I settled myself in bed, I had forgotten to call Trevor back. Oh well, I knew that phone call would result in an argument. If necessary, he would have tried calling again; I will just call him tomorrow.

Robert would stop by to see how Reign and I were doing from time to time. He would even bring her a lollipop because he knew it would make her day. The more he came over, the closer we became. His last visit took a hard left.

"So, T, there is something I would like to talk to you about."

"What is it, Rob?"

"I have been thinking about us trying again."

"Trying what?" I turned toward him with my eyebrows scrunched.

Reign was in her room watching her favorite cartoon while we were downstairs.

"Why are you looking like that?"

"No reason, but correct me if I am wrong, don't you have a whole girlfriend living with you? But you want to be with me?" I could not help but laugh at what he was saying.

"I have a plan for me to call it off and get her to move out."

"So basically, you want me to wait until you dump her and kick her out?" I asked, shaking my head in disbelief.

"If you are serious about a relationship with me, I'd rather you take care of your business before you start flirting with me because it's making me look at you in another light. How do I know if you won't do what you are doing right now to me? Plus, there is one major dilemma. I am still married."

I could tell he was upset, but I was only honest because I cared and respected him. I don't want to hurt him again. If things were different, I might consider rekindling the flames. But I cannot think of that right now. I focused on my daughter and getting this divorce finalized so I could move on.

Robert put his head down and started rubbing his head. I knew that meant he was frustrated. Robert used to do that when we dated in high school. He must not be happy. So many thoughts raced through my mind.

Just as I was about to hug him, I heard the sound of my baby girl racing down the stairs. I quickly stepped back.

"Hey Rob, come let me show you my new doll," Reign said excitedly.

"Oooh, you got a new doll? Oh, I must see it," Rob replied. I loved how he made Reign feel special. Since she had no friends to play with in the neighborhood, I was so happy she would start daycare on Monday.

He waited for Reign to go into the living room. "Now, back to you, mommy. Trinity, I am serious about us being together. I want the life we should have had. But, if I can be honest, I think your husband did us a favor.

"Wait, don't go there. Despite what has happened in my marriage, he is still Reign's father. I will not let you or anyone else talk badly about him. In her eyes, he is her superhero. Plus, who knows how a high school romance would have turned out? At this moment, I just need a friend and nothing more. Can you be a friend?"

"Oh, ok, my bad. Is there something you are not telling me?"

"What is that supposed to mean? I am very protective of my daughter and what she needs as a mother. But, if you are asking me if I love him, I do, but I am not in love. Those are two different things."

"I was…" he stutters.

Before he could finish his sentence, I immediately dismissed him. "Don't bother. Let's just let go off the topic of my daughter's father and what he did or did not do toward me. Besides, I was a freshman in high school when we dated, and I am not that same little girl. Also, you want me to be a stay-at-home mom, and I have done that. I want a career and to pursue my own goals and dreams.

I noticed Rob started fidgeting, and then he mumbled, "Trinity, I love you. I always have hated what happened back then." I almost drop the pot out of my hand when he utters those words. I could NEVER get this guy to open up about his feelings or even his life in general.

"But whatever you choose, I will be there. All I want is for you to be happy. You deserve it," he turned to head into the living room with Reign.

This man just left me baffled. I was so full of mixed emotions that I didn't know how to feel, let alone what to say after it happened. My judgment was blurry when it came to men. Finally, I shook the entire conversation out of my hand and finished cleaning off the table. When I finished, I headed in to see what Rob and Reign were up to. Standing at the entrance to the living room, the view of them playing with her baby daughter and Rob's doll baby voice was hilarious. It was so hard to hold in my laughter. I genuinely appreciate Rob checking on Reign and spending time with her, especially since everything had happened between her dad and me.

As I watched them play on the floor, it made me wonder if Rob was right. I asked myself if I should consider a relationship with him or if it was too soon. It's all too confusing, and my focus was on what was best for Reign. "Trinity, you are in a vulnerable state. Stop trying to relive your past. You are a mother now," I said to myself.

"Mommy, Mommy," Reign yelled, breaking me out of my trance. "Come play with us," Reign shouted. I turned toward Reign. "It's time for you to get cleaned up and ready for bed. Go wash your hands, sweetie."

"Okay, mommy. Bye, Rob."

"Bye, Reign," Rob replied as he waved bye. He then helped me clean up Reign's toys.

While she went to take a shower, I walked Rob to the door, and we said our goodbyes. I gave Rob a heads-up that Trevor will be coming to visit Reign, so stopping by might not be a good idea. I could tell he was in his feelings, but Reign's feelings trump everyone's. After Rob left, Reign and I spent mommy-daughter time the rest of the night. We ended the day with a movie and popcorn.

Chapter Eight

TURN OF EVENTS

10 MONTHS LATER

TURN OF EVENTS
10 MONTHS LATER

Trevor called to see if it was ok for him to visit Reign before he left for a detailed job in Canada, so of course, I agreed to the visit and even let him stay at the house.

Reign and I decided to prepare for her dad's visit. His company was planning to open a new office out there. It had been two months shy of a year since we separated. I had sent the divorce papers twice, and he still didn't sign them. He wanted to play and then come back home. Do not get it twisted; I am not for it, and my life is not a game. I shook my head, hoping it would stop the constant overthinking. I refused to let Trevor's affairs and lies contaminate me and affect my future. It's time to start a new chapter in my life.

Unlike Trevor, I decided to let him stay in the house but in a separate room. Despite how I felt, our daughter's happiness comes first. This would allow us to get the divorce papers taken care of. As I folded up the clothes, Reign came running in. "Mommy, I am so excited. I can't wait until Daddy gets here. I have so many things planned for us to do. But first, can we make a cake for his birthday?"

"Slow down, baby. Yes, you can make him a cake. Once I finish cleaning up, we will do it."

"Can we add sprinkles on it," she asked as she jumped up and down.

"Yes, whatever you like," I giggle.

After we finished making the cake, Reign went into the living to watch her cartoons and play with her toys until her dad arrived. Three hours later, Trevor called to let me know that he was outside. I opened the door and watched as he unloaded his things. As he approached me, I told him to be quiet so that he could surprise her. Trevor snuck up from behind her and picked her up. "Daddy! Daddy, you made it."

"I told you that I was coming to see my number 1 girl". Reign gave her dad a huge hug.

"Daddy, we have got a surprise for you," Reign said as she excitedly looked at me. "Mommy, can we get Daddy's surprise now?"

"Sure, can you help me?"

"Ok, Daddy, close your eyes. We will be right back."

Trevor let out a chuckle. "Yes, ma'am."

About 5 minutes later, Reign and I re-entered the living room with the cake that she made with many lit candles. Then, she began singing the Happy Birthday song while walking toward her dad with the cake in her hand.

"Ok, Daddy, open your eyes and make a wish," she said with delight. Trevor obliged Reign's wishes. "Daddy, do you like the cake we made?".

"Yes, baby, it's pretty. I have to take a picture of this amazing cake." Reign's eyes lit up with enjoyment.

"Alright, I will take it and get everyone a slice. After that, you have to get ready for bed because it's getting late."

"Aww," she said as she lowered her eyes.

"It's ok, chipmunk. When you wake up in the morning, I will be right here."

After putting Reign to bed in my room, I showed Trevor where he would be sleeping. "I thought that I would be sleeping with you," he said with a slight grin on his face.

"Well, you thought wrong. Here is your towel and washcloth. The bathroom is down the hall on the right," I said as I turned to leave the room.

"Trinity, thank you for letting me stay here and for making that cake. I know that you didn't have to do any of this."

"Well, we are still married, and I am still going to uphold my vow to God. Plus, Reign is ecstatic to spend time with you, so no need to thank me." Then I turned to walk out.

Trevor grabbed my arm as I was trying to leave. "I am sorry for what I did, and I wish that I could go back and change it. I want my marriage. That is the reason why I came here."

He did not give his visit 24 hours before dropping the I want my marriage comment.

"Ok, Trevor, good night," I said as I yanked my hand from his and walked out of the room.

The next day we spent quality time together as a family. Reign really enjoyed all of the attention and going to the amusement park. I must admit, spending time as a family made me miss Trevor a little bit. We did have some great moments in our marriage. He still knew what to do to make me smile when I tried so hard to be mad and cold. I did not see how this man could do so much to me but still be able to soften my heart toward him. Maybe I was just crazy or a fool in love; either way, I will not spoil my baby happiness of having both of her parents, especially since Trevor would be leaving in a couple of days.

After dinner, Trevor and Reign played until she passed out. I really enjoyed looking in from a distance; it felt like old times. I watched as he picked her up, took her to her room, and then kissed her on the cheek. This is the man I used to know, the one who puts family first.

When Reign was two, we would tag team to get her clean after eating spaghetti. Once she was in bed, we would plan to spend quality time together, and every time, we flopped on the couch and dozed off in each other's arms. You would have thought there was a whole basketball team we were up against. Sometimes, I believed that Reign had three people inside of her because she kept going and going, like the energizer bunny. She is my birth control pill.

As Trevor creeps out of Reign's room, I slowly back up as he closes her room door. Reign is a deep sleeper. However, since her dad has been here, she would wake up at the sound of a pin drop. So we headed back downstairs like two teenagers sneaking out without waking my parents when the coast was cleared. When we returned to the living room, we flocked on the sofa simultaneously. We looked at each other and laughed. Finally, Trevor turned to watch the game, and I decided to get a little work done.

I know you might think it's strange that we are not spending time talking to each other, even after Trevor's undying profession of love for me and wanting his family. I am used to this; he thinks his words made me believe him. I know my husband. He lies so well that he makes himself believe them. The lies caused others to believe him, too. This man could sell a flat tire with holes in it to anyone who does not know him. That's just how much he is at being a professional liar. I honestly don't believe he even knows when he is lying.

Out of nowhere, Trevor's hand reached for mine as he pulled me closer to him. We kissed tentatively, passionately, and then tenderly. He pulled my dress up over my head, and I felt the tiny sparks of static dancing over my skin. I'm not sure whether they're from my sweater or if they're from where his hands gently glided over my skin. Either way, it's a captivating feeling and causes me to shiver in complete satisfaction and ecstasy. His lips press against mine with intense passion and affection as his hands journey all over my body, leaving a trail of sparks on their way. Finally, I could no longer help myself and gave in.

"Trinity, I meant what I said; I want my family back. I am sorry for what I did to you. I know I am going to have to regain your trust, and I am willing to do it."

"Trevor, I am going to ask you again, and I need you to be honest with me. Is that girl out of our life for good?"

"Yes, she is. I promise you." And then we continued to kiss.

I knew that I should take those words with a grain of salt, but because I loved him so much, I would ever so often get blinded by his lies. I am not saying that I totally forget the things he does or has said. It's hard to put in words, but I don't think anyone would understand. I loved my husband unconditionally. Although I knew he was not perfect, neither was I. My prayers and faith helped me do this because of the man I knew he could be.

My aunt always said that every saint has a past, and every sinner has a future. Besides, my husband was family, and we both knew the ups and downs of our marriage. Everything was good one minute, and the next, they were screwing you over and no longer talking. As a believer, I needed to fight through the challenges in my marriage through the power of Christ.

"Ok, Trevor, we will move back when you come back from your work trip. He kissed me and then laid down and went to sleep. As I lay down to get comfortable, doubt ran through me about doing the right thing. I let out a deep sigh and closed my eyes.

The two months came really quickly. I could not believe it was the day for Reign and me to move. We spent time trying to get used to the mommy-daughter team for the last year. I know that Reign is excited, but I couldn't help but have mixed feelings. I don't want my daughter to think that I am weak and need a man, nor do I want to take her through a yo-yo effect. Just the thought of being moving is giving me heart palpitations and uneasiness. I feel like I am on a roller coaster as a dramatic climb starts to slow as I reach the acme of the structure. The feeling of fear of not knowing what's my future, it makes me second guess if I have made the right decision. Just then, out of nowhere, the infectious laughter of my daughter snapped me out of the darkness of my mind.

Something about that little bright-eyed girl's laughter is unexplainable. It was like magic or the summer breeze that blows through your hair while walking on the beach. It was a moment in time that you wanted to be in. Her laughter and smile confirmed that I had done the right thing for her, so I will try and do my best to make these couple of days pleasant. This is the moment I wish I had watched my uncle a little more closely when he played poker. I think that I would have probably had a master poker face.

I did not want to interrupt their father-daughter time, so I focused on unpacking and making this place a little homier. So, I decided to call Giselle. She always knew what to say to help me stop overthinking. Since I was a little girl, I have been an over-thinker. I would analyze so many outcomes that it would become a problem, and one would think I loved having issues. Being a lawyer may have been my true calling in life.

Giselle and I talk about everything under the sun. One would have thought we had not spoken in a month, but we just talk yesterday. Giselle told me she was having a baby with her son's father. I didn't know what to think, but I knew I would support my friend. How much of a friend would I be if I were not honest with her? I knew she didn't want to hear it; what woman would? And I was not about to do it either, especially while she is pregnant.

So, I guess that made me a horrible friend. She seemed happy; I didn't want to take this moment from her or stress her and the baby. I just listen to her brag about their fourth go-round into this relationship. If things did not turn out how Giselle planned, I would be here to comfort her and love on her. She has had my back so many times through this ordeal with Trevor. Those late-night phone calls with me pouring my heart out about how Trevor made me feel like it was me and I was not good for him. Giselle was right there, talking me off the ledge.

Just then, Trevor walked into the room and kissed me on the cheek. He told me to tell Giselle hi, then headed for the shower. Ten minutes later, Giselle and I said our goodbyes, and I decided to check on Reign before lying down. I slowly opened the door and peeped my head in to see my little princess sleeping peacefully with her red teddy bear. I left her door halfway open in case she woke and got scared. I headed back to the room and lay down but was immediately startled by Trevor's phone constantly ringing. "Someone needs to get in touch with Trevor; his phone keeps going off," I thought.

I reached over to the nightstand to see if it was work, but instead, it was her. Besides telling my husband to leave his family, that little girl does not understand what it takes in a marriage. My heart stopped, and I gasped as I read the text messages on his phone between him and his mistress about an unborn child. As I was sitting on the bed, with red in my eyes, focusing on the bathroom door where Trevor was taking a shower, my anxiety grew. The tears, mixed with rage and anger, ran down my eyes. The thoughts raced through my mind.

Should I email all the messages and pictures to all his co-workers and boss? "Who is this man I lay next to every night? How could he lie and hurt me like this again? He promised me this was a new start from the pain and suffering and hurt he put me through," I whispered to myself. Then the door to the bathroom opened, and it interrupted my thought. As Trevor walked into the room, he noticed I had his phone in my hand. Looking at my expression, he probably realized I knew his big secret.

The more I thought it all through, the more the rage flowed through me like lava. I could feel the pulse in my veins; I threw his phone at his face. I did not realize I had hit him until he grabbed his head. As I clenched my fist together, I began pacing the room, trying to get my thoughts together.

"What the hell is this, Trevor? Is she pregnant? By you? YOU said it was over, and she was out of our lives. Answer me!"

Trevor's eyes darted, and then he looked at me. "Um, yes," he said as his voice cracked.

"Are you fucking kidding me! I quit my job and packed up our daughter for this bullshit." I begin to pace the room again and shake my head in disbelief.

Stopping abruptly and directly in front of him, pointing my finger in his face, "I asked you when you came to visit, and you lied. That was your opportunity for you to tell me the truth. I don't know who the fuck you are! I don't want you around our daughter, and I don't want you around me. I pray to God that she finds a husband better than you. I hate you, and I wish I never met you."

I admit that I lost all of my holier-than-thou, God-fearing, loving wife spirit. He brought something out of me that I thought I had left in Florida. Kiesha, my old college roommate, tried to warn me about him and the change I had made. I cannot believe this BOY lied to me again.

"Why didn't you sign the damn divorce papers?! Why couldn't you just leave me alone? You got your damn mistress pregnant. Do you even know if it's even yours?"

"I am not sure."

"You are not sure? Are you serious? If you could not trust the chick, why would you not use protection?"

He just sat there, not saying anything.

"You are so stupid. She got just what she wanted from you, a fucking check."

I could no longer look at him. I kept asking question after question while packing my clothes. Trevor's answers were not satisfying, and it only made me angrier. Finally, I told him that I had wanted another child all these years, and he kept telling me no. So many thoughts kept going through my mind. The more I kept thinking, the faster I started packing.

Trevor's phone was still ringing, but he dared not answer it. I stopped in my tracks of packing and turned and grabbed the phone out of his hand.

"Hello," I could not hide my attitude.

"Can I speak to Trevor," the female voice on the other line replied.

"He is currently busy, but how can I help you?"

"This does not concern you."

I was taken aback because this chick thinks she has the power or is on my level. First, I had to look at the phone, then at Trevor.

"Lil girl, if you don't take that damn tone and drop it down several feet, I know something. Now, let me correct you on something. Anything regarding Trevor is my damn business. And that baby that you are carrying will be my business as long as I am married to him."

This little girl seems incredibly naive or perhaps delusional. She truly believes that I would not be involved in this situation or in the child's life, all while still being married to the unfaithful man I unfortunately call my husband.

"See, you just prove how young and dumb you are. That is something only an immature home wrecker would say. The sad part is that you are going to be the mother to that baby."

Then, she proceeded to assure me that her child would be well-behaved and that she didn't require anything from us. She also made a point of mentioning that she never called me or attempted to confront me about my husband. I found it ironic that she was painting herself as the victim when they both was equally involved in the affair. I couldn't help but laugh at her remark.

"Don't concern yourself with how I handle my husband with his infidelity. You finally got one thing right: I called you, but you knew he was married and still pursued him. The issue I have with YOU is your disrespect and lack of apology. Now, you want to play the victim. You lay up with a married man, knowing he refuses to sign the divorce papers. That bullshit you mention fighting, sweetie, you know where we live. So, any time you feel confident, ring the doorbell," and then I hung the phone up.

I immediately started packing Reign's and my things. I was packing so fast that you would have thought I was trying to win a race. Then I went out the door and put our stuff in the car. I went up and down the stairs what felt like a hundred times, trying to avoid looking at Trevor while he sat on the sofa, but really, it was only two; with all our things, it felt like it. Finally, Trevor decided to follow me on my third trip out. I had no idea what made him do that, but he still did not have enough of my mouth.

"Trinity, can we please talk?" he stammered out the words. I turned to him with a narrow-eyed and crinkled nose. It was an out-of-body experience because I did not realize that I was doing it. Trevor stood there with his shoulders hunched over, looking at the ground. I am not sure what he was looking at because it was pitch black in the early morning. If I had to guess, it was around 1 am.

"Really? Talk? Trevor, what more do we need to talk about? I think that we covered everything. YOUR MISTRESS IS HAVING YOUR BABY. Yep, I think that covers it," I said as I stared at him without blinking my eyes. I turned my head and went back to sorting everything in the trunk of my car.

"Trinity, it's late, and Reign is sleeping. So why not wait to leave in the morning, although I prefer you all not to leave."
I stopped again in the midst of putting Reign's toys into the car, "Trevor, why did you not tell me she was pregnant? Why did you lie?" I asked, and then I closed the trunk.

Trevor had trouble maintaining eye contact with me, "I knew you would not come or try to save our marriage. So I left her, and later, she told me that she was pregnant."

I turned and walked back into the house and just flopped on the sofa. You would have thought I lost my balance as hard as I sat down. I sat there and stared at him with my arms and legs crossed. I watch as he walks in and closes the front door. Then he turned on the security system as if he was trying to prevent me from escaping. Then he made his way toward our black loveseat and sat in silence.

I wondered if he remembered he asked if we could talk. I hoped he didn't think the outside discussion was the talk. I continued to stare at him while tapping my feet, waiting for him to start. Five minutes later, the room was still silent, and at this point, my eyelids were trying to give way.

"I am going to bed, GOODNIGHT," I said as I got up and walked up the spiral stairs.

As I made my way into the room, sleep began to get taken over by my rage. The flood of mixed emotions started to take control of me. One minute, I was angry, and the next, I was sad and ashamed. How can I look at my daughter and not feel embarrassed? What will I tell my family and friends as I put my head in my hand? I began judging myself before anyone else had the chance. As soon as I sat down on our king-size pillow-top mattress, the tears started to flow like a raging river. I quickly put my head into the pillow to muffle the sound because I did not want to wake Reign up at 3 am. I think she had seen enough of her mommy crying for a lifetime.

My thoughts have found their way back into my head; the more they came, the more I cried. When Reign was two, I tried to get Trevor to agree to have another child. He had so many excuses as to why we should not have another child, but three years later, he had one on the way with his mistress. I guess I was not good enough. You have asked me before; I would have done anything for this man. I made him my world, and he knew I was hesitant to do so from my previous relationship. I took a chance on love, but I was wrong. I feel like my body is being deprived of oxygen right now. I don't want to suffocate in this lie of a marriage. Finally decided to try to go to sleep because making a rash decision will impact Reign.

I guess it was not enough because Trevor came up the stairs to console me. At first, I did not mind it, but the longer he did, the more my pain turned into anger. Then I pushed back from him because, in my mind, he did not get the right to console me. Trevor did not get the right to jump in and play the superhero, the knight in shining armor, the loving husband. NO! Not tonight, not ever. He was the reason for all of this, the reason why I was feeling that way.

"Trevor, I'm good. Just leave me alone, please."

"Trinity, I was just trying to help."

"Help me by erasing all that you have done. Help me by taking the pain and embarrassment that I currently feel." There was a long, awkward pause between both of us. "Good night, Trevor." And then I laid down with my back turned toward him. Finally, I doze off after lying in the dark for a while.

As the sunlight shone through the corners of my beige curtains, I could hear the birds chirping outside. Why were they so happy? What made them sing such a happy tune? There is nothing to be satisfied with, ugh. I cannot understand how I gave my heart to be broken by such a lousy man. How could the one who made me happy make me feel so sad? The love that brought so much pleasure now brings misery. How can I continue in the marriage with a child out of wedlock from his mistress?

"Get it together, Trinity. Reign will be bouncing in here soon, and you do not want her to see you crying and sad." I tried to give myself a pep talk, but it was not helping. And whoever said sleeping the pain off will help is a liar. The pain of last night was still there. Unfortunately, my pity party abruptly stopped because I could hear the sound of pitter-patter.

"Good morning, skipping Mommy," Reign said as she skipped in with her bubbly personality.

"Good morning, baby," I said as I kissed her on her forehead.

"Mommy, mommy, can I have banana blueberry pancakes!" she said as she bounced up and down.

"Okay, give me a few minutes, and I will come downstairs and make them for you."

"Okay, Dokey," Reign said as she turned and left my room door.

I preferred lying in bed, but I had a daughter who needed her mother, so reluctantly, I got out of bed and went into the bathroom to freshen up before heading downstairs.

As I descended the stairs, I noticed Trevor and Reign sitting on the sofa watching cartoons. I did not want to interrupt their bonding time, so I headed to the kitchen to make some pancakes. I did not want to talk to Trevor. I didn't want to say something I couldn't take back, nor did I want to make a permanent decision based on temporary emotions. But I knew that I would eventually have to talk to him, and I didn't wish for Reign to feel any negativity.

I prepared everyone's plate and then walked into the living room. "Alrighty, you two, breakfast is now served."
Reign did not hesitate. She quickly jumped out of her father's lap and ran to the table to eat.

"Thanks, Trinity," Trevor said in a monotone as he sat at the table.

"No problem. Reign made a special request this morning anyway," I replied in a nonchalant tone and sat down.

"Trevor, I think you and Reign should have a daddy-daughter day. And we will talk when you all get back." I did not want Reign to know what was going on between her daddy and me, and I admit it was hard to hold all my anger in.

"Yes, daddy…daddy-daughter day!" as she jumped up and down in her seat.

"Sure, anything for my baby girl," he said as he looked at Reign and gave her a smile before taking a sip of his OJ.

While they were out on their daddy-daughter date, I cried, I screamed, and then I prayed. I wanted so much to call my aunt or Giselle, but I knew they would only add fuel to the fire. I could clearly hear them saying, "Leave and get your child support and alimony," but honestly, I did not want the easy way out. I wanted what was best for my daughter and me. "Lord, please give me strength and let Your will be done. Please walk with me and guide the words that come out of my mouth." I sat on the sofa, just staring into space for what seemed like a few minutes, but eventually, it was hours.

Just as I was getting up from the sofa, Reign and Trevor walked in. She ran to me and gave me the biggest hug.
"Reign, take your things to your room to play with them while I talk to you, Dad."

"Okay, Mommy."

"Trevor, let's talk," I said as I sat back down on the sofa with my legs crossed and arms folded.

"Trinity, I'm sorry. If I could take it all back, I would."

"But you can't. So, save it," I said as I rudely interrupted him.

Trevor started to explain the situation and what had happened. I was not too concerned about the mistress and the baby; I had to know why the infidelity occurred in the first place.

If he was unhappy, why didn't he just say something instead of confiding in a little girl the same age as my baby brother? He could have upgraded instead of dealing with a homey-looking girl. I still felt like he was lying about some of the questions.

"Trevor, you are leaving next week for work, so while you are gone for the three months, Reign and I will stay here. That will give me some time to figure out what I want to do."

"Okay, Trinity. I'm sorry. I love you," Trevor said.

I got up without any words and went into the room to process the conversation. While Trevor was home, I did my best to avoid him the remaining time. We only talked when it was about legal matters or Reign. He slept on the sofa while I slept in the room. We were married roommates. When Reign was around, I would interact and play the happy family role. I am not a person who can fake it, so you know that it was eating me up to act like everything was good. But I will do anything for my baby.

While Trevor was gone, Reign and I got into a bit of a routine of our own. I love it when it's just the two of us. She even started playing tennis, and I started a new job. The only time I think of the issue in my marriage is when Trevor calls to apologize or give me an update about his child. Today's call was a little different. First, I had to focus on calming him down. He told me he received a letter that he was being put on child support. "That was fast," I said as I thought to myself. The baby is not even a month old. I hate to say I told you so, but I kept it to myself. I just reassured him that we would get through it.

Reign and I awaited Trevor's return, speaking with him every day while he was away. As the days of his return approached, my anxiety intensified, knowing that soon he would be back under the same roof. I hadn't contemplated my next move and had been trying to bury my emotions deep within, almost as if I were in denial.

Three Weeks Later

Trevor came home a couple of days before Reign started school, so I suggested we take a weekend beach trip to Maryland. That has always been a place where I could clear my head and get away from the stress of the world. There were a lot of happy memories there.

The one thing that I can give him is that he is a great dad, but unfortunately, he just sucks at being a husband. Nevertheless, there is something I see in him that gives me hope, which causes me to keep lowering my defenses to try again. But like I said before, no rash decisions.

So, the next day, after breakfast, we packed a couple of things and drove an hour outside DC to our beach house in Cape Saint Claire, Maryland. After celebrating one of our anniversaries there, Trevor and I decided to invest in a timeshare four years later. The view was so captivating that we could not resist buying a place in the area. Since then, we have gone every summer.

Reign quietly jumped out of the car and headed into the house. I followed behind her while Trevor unloaded the vehicle. As usual, Reign beat everyone, changing into their swimwear. I wondered why she couldn't do that when she got up for school. Every morning, I have to repeat myself at least five times before she even gets out of bed.

"Come on, Mommy, let's go!"

"Okay, calm down, little one. We have to wait for Daddy to change, and then we will head down to the beach."

"Reign, are you trying to leave me?"

"Oh no daddy," Reign said with a disappointing tone. You would have thought her dad had said we were not going until later. While he changed, we packed some water and snacks to enjoy out on the beach. Once Trevor had changed, we headed down to the beach for plenty of fun in the sun.

As we walked closer to the beach, the visibility of the seawater was blue and beautiful as it sparkled in the warm sun. The beach was not crowded, and only a few people were there, so we had a lot of space to set up. I decided to read a book and look on as Trevor and Reign built a sandcastle. Well, at least the initial attempt was supposed to be a sandcastle. The beach was peaceful, aside from the delicate crash of waves against the sand, the faint call of hungry seagulls, and the kids' laughter.

As I sat and enjoyed my solitude, I closed my eyes and listened to the soothing sounds around me. I could feel the warm rays of the sun against my face. It all felt so serene.

A few hours passed, and the sun started to dip below the horizon of the ocean waves. Finally, we decided to pack up and head back to the house for dinner. It had been a long day, so we decided to make it a pizza night.

Reign was so tired when we got home that she fell fast asleep after bathing. It worked out well for us because Trevor and I planned to video chat with my Godmother. I told her my Godmother every time that I get, that my mom got something right when she picked her to be my Godmother. Trevor loved and gave her the utmost respect as well. When he met her, he could not believe that she had never cursed or drunk any liquor or wine. Not to mention, when you walked into her house, you could feel God's presence. I'm not trying to say my Godmother is a saint, and she doesn't have trials or tribulations. I might take that back. She is a saint to me, in my eyes. But really, she is what I have strived to be since this ordeal. The way she carried herself when problems arose.

"Trevor, are you ready to call my Godmother?"

"Yes," he reluctantly answered. I picked up the computer and facetimed her.

After a few rings, the picture of a beautiful, middle-aged woman with a welcoming smile appeared, "Hey T, how are you all doing?"

"We are okay, just taking it one day at a time. How are you doing?"

"I am good; I cannot complain. I just finished my meeting, but we can talk about that later. First, let's discuss some important matters. How are you all doing? Hi Trevor, how are you?"

"I am doing okay," Trevor responded. He did not want to deal with our marriage's issues. Unfortunately, Trevor did not have a choice. Either he faces it, or it's a wrap. The last time we tried counseling, he lied to the minster while IN THE CHURCH.

Trevor and I took turns explaining each other's side and point of view. She listened to us talk for about thirty minutes without interruption. Then, my Godmother would interject with a cough when she felt it would lead to an argument between us or over-talking one another. You know the cough you got in church when your mom wanted you to be civilized, or she would take you into the bathroom if you embarrassed her?

"Trevor, when we as women try to convey our anxiety, we will bring up facts, and our tone might change because we are passionate. I understand, Trevor, that it might have caused you to feel attacked. I am not saying it's okay; I just want you to understand. In Trinity's mind, she is searching for compassion and understanding, but all Trevor hears is you pointing out his shortcomings. Trinity, this makes Trevor want to either shut down or respond defensively."

"Trinity, you can let the hurt and pain harden your heart, but if Trevor is trying to correct his wrongs and both want to fix your marriage, Trinity, you must trust and forgive him. But Trevor, you have to understand it will take time for her to move past what has happened, and you must figure out what you must do to soften the heart and get her to forgive and trust you again."

My Godfather came in and sat in on the conversation. "I agree, sweetie," he said as he kissed her on the cheek. It is a testament to a long-lasting 30-year marriage, and they are still in love like two teenagers.

"Trevor, most of the time, a woman is not trying to win the argument or disagree in a conversation. Sometimes, she is crying out for love and understanding from her husband. You would want her to come to you rather than to the arms of another man or a messy girlfriend about how she is feeling or your marriage. The reason why she brings up facts is to validate her point. So, Trevor, stop feeling like the victim or like Trinity is heartless. You must see yourself as a perpetrator of hurt, not the victim of rejection. The only thing self-pity will do is contaminate your growth and prayer."

I watched as my Godmother looked at her husband with so much love. She reached over, grabbed his hand, and looked back at us. "T, you have to give Trevor a chance. And both of you must pray together and for one another. Communication is the key to success, and it is also important to keep God in the center of your marriage and family. So, before we go, let's pray." We all bow our heads, and my Godfather begins to pray. Afterward, we said our goodbyes.

After that talk with my Godparents, I felt a sense of release. This moment was the beginning of a new start. Not to sound corny, but Trevor and I just discovered that we are expecting our 2nd child together might be our sign of a new start. Also, we will be moving to the West Coast because of my recent promotion. I could breathe again, smile, and be happy.

On our way home from Maryland, Trevor's baby's mother called with an instantaneous attitude. I believe she is bitter. I could hear her just fussing on the other end of the phone. She is acting like they are together or married, from her demands. So, I grabbed Trevor's phone and tried to reason with her for the kids' sake, but it did not go over well. She claimed he told her life would be better if she were with him. And everything after that was blah blah blah. So, finally, after about five minutes of her rambling, I cut her off.

"Well, if he said all that to you, can you go with me and help me get a divorce? Then you can be together." I refuse to go back and forth about a man or husband. My focus now are by kids and peace of mind. I guess she was surprised by my comment because she refuses to go with me to help me get out of my marriage. If you are married in DC and have a child, you must be separate for a year before you can get a divorce, unless there is infidelity or abuse.

"So, what is the point of you saying all that? You and Trevor need to learn how to communicate better for your daughter's sake. You all cannot co-parent effectively if every time ya'll talk, it's an argument. "

Despite her lingering defensiveness and bitterness, I made a conscious decision to de-escalate the situation by taking the high road. I am determined not to let her undermine all the effort and personal development I've put in.

"Okay, bye," I said and hung up the phone.

I looked at Trevor and asked what that was all about. He looked confused. I didn't know if he was confused or back to habitual lying. We talked the entire trip home, and he decided to call her back. It was funny how she started stuttering and changing things. Before long, Trevor and her back at arguing back and forth. I could not get a word in. Finally, after ten minutes of listening to them going back and forth, I screamed and told him to hang up the phone. Trevor was getting to a point where it could be detrimental. So, I tried to calm him down. Things still were unresolved between him and me, but I was drained.

After that incident, I decided to pack our things and leave. I refuse to go through what I went through last year. Trevor tried to calm me down and reassure that there is nothing going on between them. His first action to prove it, he was going to take her to court. So that she cannot continue using the baby as a pawn. I agree to try and save our marriage. You may wonder why I stayed in this marriage. If I had a clear answer, I would tell you. But I was a little unsure, and every time I tried to leave, God did something to make me stay.

The following Sunday, Reign and I went to church. The Bishop was not speaking today; there was a guest speaker. This evangelist, the woman of God, walked over to me and said, "God told me to tell you that you are consumed with despair, and the issue you are going through is over. You no longer have to worry about it anymore." As she walked away, I cried and dropped to my knees because I knew she was talking about my marriage. It scared Reign a little bit because she began to cry.

The next day, I got a phone call for a job offer. It was one that I could not pass up. And I was so surprised by it because this was the week Reign, and I was supposed to be move to West Coast. "Really, God? You know I was planning on leaving, and then you gave me my dream job," I said as I looked up to the sky.

For the past few days, I've found myself grappling with a weighty decision – whether to remain and work on salvaging my marriage or to part ways. Despite my assurance to Trevor that I would stay, I couldn't deny my inner turmoil and uncertainty – until now.

Well, I guess Reign and I will be in DC after all and no relocating. The job will give me the experience and time to figure out my marriage. I figured God was telling me to work on my marriage. We would have a long talk when Trevor returned, but I was focused on getting back to Trinity right now. The person I was before was a wife and mother. It's time I focus on my career goals and continue my relationship with God. I am not doing this just for myself but for my daughter. I don't want her to think a man determines who you are or that she has to put herself on the shelf.

Once Reign was in bed, we sat down and discussed our marriage. We decided that divorce would not be a topic of discussion. We realized it would take much work to repair our marriage. Trevor finally realized that the process might be slow, but we will get through as long as we work, are willing, and center God in our marriage.

Two years later, we were still working on our marriage but were in a much better place. Reign is so in love with her baby brother and little half-sister. Now, my world is complete. Trevor won his court order visitation, and the kids have grown closer to their half-sister. Yet, I would be lying if I said I still didn't struggle with the infidelity and child out of wedlock. Still, I managed not to let it overtake me or my marriage.

In the new space that I am in, I thought it was time to put my feelings aside and do what was best for my kids. I decided to talk to Trevor about calling his baby mama and discussing boundaries for the kids' sake. If we decided to put the baby in an activity, I wanted us to be in the same space without drama. I was not trying to have tea and crumpets or become a shopping buddy, and I just wanted her to understand that she is welcome to come if we put her daughter in any sports or activities. I cannot replace her as the mother, but kids want their parents to be present and to cheer them on.

At first, Trevor was hesitant, but I explained to him that was my only focus and nothing else. I was prepared for her to come out of left field with some BS, so I stepped outside to call her, but I prayed before I did it.

"Lord, please do not let my emotions control me. Help me be your best representation and do what is pleasing in your eyes. "

This girl answered the phone with an attitude, so I knew this would be one of God's tests. I shook my head as I explained to her the nature of my call and how we needed to do what was best for the kids. This girl kept going back to my husband about what he was or was not doing, how he needed to stay out of the club and be a husband, blah blah blah. She almost got me to go there, but I quietly stopped myself and explained this call was not about Trevor. Let me worry about Trevor since she said she didn't want to be him. I asked her several times to focus on why I called because Trevor was not the reason.

After twenty minutes of going back and forth and keeping my composure, I finally said, "Since you do not want to have anything to do with our family activities, do not come to my husband about not inviting you to anything again. And you have a blessed life."

When I got off the phone, I was so proud of myself. Usually, Trevor's Baby Mama would get me out of my character, but I stayed true to the plan. I walked back into the house and told Trevor what had happened and how she tried focusing on him, not the kids. He was shocked. He finally realized the kind of person this girl was and understood that I would only get involved if it affected this household. All their arguments and back and forth are between them.

It takes people to go through hell to realize what they have. My husband realizes that I have stayed true to my word. Since our first meeting, my actions have always aligned with my words.

Our family grew from one kid to three. Although we had our moments, we were happy and more in love than ever. Trevor and I felt as believers, we must fight through the challenges in marriage through the power of Christ. Even now, I admit the only way my marriage survived was with God and prayer. I do not have any other explanation. And if you ask Trevor, he will say I am the reason.

The Other WOMAN

When I first said, "I Do," I expected a happy marriage filled with joy and two kids. I envisioned both of us having a successful career and growing stronger financially and emotionally. But don't get it twisted; I knew we would have our ups and downs, but never in a million years did I expect infidelity and an outside child. Although this situation brought me to my lowest point in life and embarrassed me, it made me more vigorous and unapologetic for putting my kids and me first. No longer will I let any individual take me to that place where I would lose my confidence or self-esteem?

Although my marriage is still going strong, we still have more work. But the best part is we have a great support system. I have come out of this situation with my faith stronger in the Lord, two amazing kids, and one awesome bonus kid, and my career is blooming. I could not be in a better place.

You probably thought this book's focus was cheating and sex. You were so wrong! Although included, that was not the story's primary focus. This story is about a woman who I did not know. The woman survived the loss of a child and reclaimed her life after being on her deathbed. The woman who survived infidelity, embarrassment, and the betrayal of an outside child. The woman who was born through heartache, suffering, and significant loss. A woman whom I didn't know that had the strength or grace to become. My journey birthed a woman of power and resiliency. I have shed the old to become **THE OTHER WOMAN.**

L. S. TOPPING

About THE AUTHOR

L. S. TOPPING

About THE AUTHOR

L. S. TOPPING

THE AUTHOR

L. S. TOPPING

Meet Latoyoua Topping, MBA—a dedicated mother, wife, and visionary author seamlessly bridging the worlds of children's and women's literature. Her acclaimed children's trilogy, *The Big Move, Daddy's Big Trip,* and *Dad Returns Home,* have profoundly impacted young readers and even garnered a letter of appreciation from First Lady Michelle Obama.

A recipient of multiple children's book awards, Latoyoua combines her business acumen with a deep passion for storytelling. Now, she expands her reach to address themes that resonate with women, crafting narratives rich in empathy, wisdom, and inspiration.

THE *Other* WOMAN

L. S. TOPPING

SHEROPUBLISHING.COM

Made in the USA
Columbia, SC
19 November 2024

46578616R00080